The Hard Way Home

The Hard

Outdoor Lives

Way Home

Alaska Stories of
Adventure, Friendship,
and the Hunt

STEVE KAHN

University of Nebraska Press • Lincoln & London

Acknowledgments for the use of
copyrighted material appear on pages
207–208, which constitute an extension
of the copyright page.

Library of Congress Cataloging-in-
Publication Data

Kahn, Steve, 1954–
The hard way home: Alaska stories of
adventure, friendship, and the hunt /
Steve Kahn.
       p. cm. — (Outdoor lives series)
ISBN 978-0-8032-3268-6 (hardcover: alk.
paper)
1. Hunting—Alaska—Anecdotes.
2. Outdoor life—Alaska—Anecdotes.
I. Title.
SK49.K34 2010
799.29798—dc22
2010000152

Set in Swift EF by Kim Essman.

For Anne

For my parents, Gus and Ann Kahn

Contents

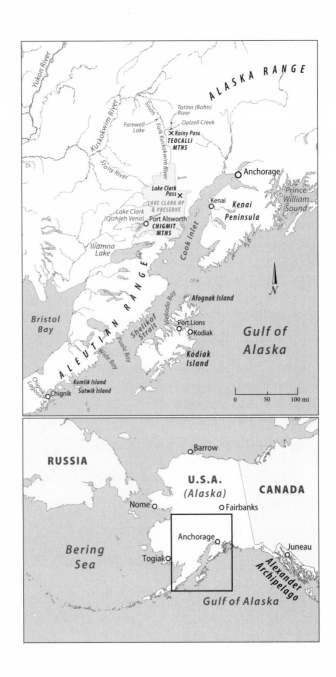

Introduction

Being born in Alaska during territorial days was none of my doing and all of my fortune. I thank my parents for deciding to live north, but do I stop there? Without my mother's family fleeing from Germany after World War II to Wisconsin, without my mother catching the eye of a young man newly enlisted in the Air Force, who knows what might have happened? When my father asked my mother to marry him, there was a catch. He told her she had to fly to Alaska first. When she stepped off the plane in Anchorage and he wasn't there to meet her, she almost turned around and got back on the same flight south—and that could have been the end of my story before it even started. The flight had been delayed, and my father had been nervously sipping coffee all morning. They found each other when he emerged from the bathroom. Within a year I was born.

I wonder sometimes how far back my connection to the outdoors goes. My father was born into a family of hunters, fishermen, and resourceful women. They were rural, hard working, small-farm folks from the upper Midwest. My maternal grandfather climbed and hiked in the German Alps before the war broke out. My mother enjoyed getting outside to pick yarrow and other herbs for the soldiers' tea when she was sent to a German youth camp. Later, in Alaska, she made countless excursions in search of Alaskan wildflowers to complete a photo album and add flowers to her garden: shooting stars, iris, Jacob's Ladder, forget-me-nots.

When I was nine years old, my family moved from the Anchorage suburbs to our homesite in the foothills of the Chugach Mountains. Running through our land was a tributary of Campbell Creek, and surrounding our home were wooded hills, trails, and wetlands. I belong to perhaps the last generation to understand such places as a child's backyard, playground, and simply a safe place to be. I had the freedom and opportunity to say "I'm going to the swamp," or "I'll be at the creek," before wandering off to explore by myself or with a friend. Even my mother checked her protective instincts and allowed me to roam at will.

The distance from the banks of the south fork of little Campbell Creek, where my fascination with the wild really took root, to my present home on the north shore of Lake Clark isn't that far really, less than two hundred miles. For me, it's been a decades-long journey from a tiny creek to the sixth-largest lake in Alaska. Like so many others, I have found it impossible to maintain a straight line from childhood to adulthood.

I grew up fishing, berry picking, and hunting, but I never considered being a big-game guide until the opportunity unfolded unexpectedly when I was in my early twenties. I was lucky to have one of the finest mentors in the business. His name was Stan Frost, and he was a man of confidence, integrity, and clearly defined values. Perhaps most critical for my schooling wasn't the knowledge of mountains and flying he shared, but his belief in my abilities and his patience with my mistakes. I worked for or alongside Stan for fourteen years, and with his encouragement earned my pilot's license and started my own outfitting business.

For almost twenty years I was a guide—it was my primary

occupation and source of adventure during my younger years—and other experiences, such as flying, crab fishing, and oil recovery work, grew from or dovetailed with the guiding. When someone asked if I wanted a job in a mill shop, on a commercial fishing boat, or as a carpenter, I said yes—as long as it didn't interfere with the spring and fall hunting seasons.

Many Alaskans enjoy jack-of-all-trades lives. We go in various directions, trying our hand at many things. There is an expansiveness to living a life that is not limited by specialization. It is empowering to be around so many folks who, when the pipes freeze or a trailer hitch breaks, think "I need a wrench or welding rod," not, "I need to call a plumber or a welder."

Some of the skills or lessons I am most grateful to have learned from guiding are not what folks might expect. When boots and packs fell apart mid-season I learned the value of an awl and needle. I became a decent chef and learned enough German to get my message across. Time on boats and in airplanes taught me the nuances of knots and control knobs.

During my years guiding and commercial fishing I kept a journal. Sometimes the entries were nothing more than "up the Earl River, saw 3 caribou, 2 black bear, 8 sheep," or "dropped a load of pots in Viekoda Bay," quickly scribbled before I zipped up my sleeping bag for the night. Occasionally the day's events, my mood, or a surge of adrenaline made for longer offerings. The journals are stained, literally, with blood, sweat, and coffee. They have been an invaluable source for writing these stories, not only for names and dates, but also as a way to return me to a place; a time; the taste of saltwater on my lips; the strain of a heavy pack.

There are challenges in arranging stories that span many years or that cannot easily be categorized under one subject. I opted finally for a loose chronological arrangement within each section, thereby offering a sense of changes happening not only within Alaska but also within myself. Still, I make liberal use of flashback and reflection—perhaps unavoidably for someone who didn't begin to write nonfiction until he was in his forties. Elements other than time bind individual stories: a longtime friendship connects several episodes through decades of adventure in "Hats Off to Hal"; in "Getting There," the urge to push on while traveling in the bush links incidents separated by years; while the transformation of my love of fishing propels the narrative in "One Last Cast."

The book is divided into three sections. The first, *Ranging Out,* provides the background for my interest in the outdoors, and includes adventures in boats and airplanes. The stories in section two, *Guiding Days,* are focused on my early to mid-adult years spent as a big-game guide. *Settled In*, the final section, deals with my life since then, living on Lake Clark. I have given up guiding, commercial fishing, and trapping, but still engage in subsistence hunting and fishing.

My past goes with me every time I step onto a trail or into a boat or airplane. My experiences in the far reaches of Alaska are diverse and full of humorous, poignant, complex, and simple moments. I hope these pages offer more than stories of hunting, trapping, and fishing. I have attempted a portrayal of northern life—my love and connection to Alaska, its conflicts, wild places, plants, animals, and people.

One

Ranging Out

One Last Cast

1

Many go fishing all their lives without knowing that it is not fish they are after.—H. D. THOREAU

I remember gazing into a mountain stream near Turnagain Pass. Minute air bubbles formed along the backs of polished granite boulders hunched at the bottom, then rose in a swirl of motion to the surface. My little hands held tight their first fishing pole: a willow branch rigged with a piece of string from the glove box, a safety pin, and a half-ripe cranberry. I was four years old, maybe five. My folks tell me I was more interested in fishing than a potty stop.

Alaska proved to be paradise for a boy who loved to fish. My memories of our frequent family road trips along the Alcan Highway are fixed with two passions: counting animals and spotting places to fish. Of course, this meant a request from me to stop at every lake, creek, culvert, or bridge we passed. "Soon, Stevie," my Dad would say, as the dust billowed behind our Rambler to settle on the quickly passing water that held, I imagined, swarms of ravenous grayling and trout. When I did fish (and it seemed like once out of every hundred opportunities), I got more bites from gnats and mosquitoes than from anything with gills and a dorsal fin.

When, in 1956, my folks purchased a homesite in the hills above Anchorage, with a creek running through the property, those ninety-nine untapped possibilities flowed through my dreams, twisted, cut, sparkled, and finally co-alesced into one stream: the south fork of Little Campbell Creek. Except during the spring when the creek would darken and swell, its waters were bubbly and sweet, and seldom deeper than my knees. The creek cut a silvery slice through birch and white spruce. I could step over it in a few spots, jump across it in many places, and wade from bank to bank with impunity.

Little Campbell Creek held small miracles in its folds. Not just fish, these were sleek goldenfin Dolly Varden sporting a splash of amber along their small-scaled sides. They found many places to hide. Sometimes, especially on warm afternoons, they rested under a spruce log bridge where two almost imperceptible channels lay. Or they found shelter under cut banks, an aqueous world of roots and shadows, which I glimpsed from downstream on the opposite side, or by leaning oh-so-slowly over a mossy overhang to peer below.

I baited my single hook with a salmon egg. I learned not to let the point of the hook pierce all the way through the orange-red rubbery globe. There was little need to cast. The line was more an extension of the arm, a gentle swing to will the bait to a spot just beyond reach.

I would fish for hours, alone most of the time. Though sharing toys came easily, my personal space was different. An only child, I relished time to myself. A friend's mother tells how I would come over to play with her son, but when the neighborhood boys started showing up, she would suddenly notice that I'd disappeared.

One childhood friend spent his time pushing toy trucks around his yard, a rumble-whir sound in his throat as he built overpasses and brought mini-highways up to grade. Another friend held a fascination with model cars and ships, spending countless hours redesigning a Model A's suspension or the gun turrets on a battleship. I had a yellow dump truck and model cars and airplanes sitting on my dresser, but usually the waves that pulled me were not of sound or air, but gentle riffles coursing thinly over stones and gravel or teething through the twisted roots of a spruce.

Dangling a salmon egg on a hook in front of a six-inch trout for hours until the fish either bit or darted downstream like a bullet mesmerized me. I wasn't old enough to define passion or know what forms it could take. It was just life, not divided yet into parts. The creek: a place to dam, to wade, to float wooden boats, but mostly a place to fish.

Mom would fry up my catch any time of the day I asked. There was never enough for a meal for the family, just a Dolly or two, hanging from a forked willow branch that I proudly hauled into the kitchen. I ate the tender flesh that peeled away easily from the delicate backbone, savored the crisp tail that was fried in butter until it was almost translucent. Sometimes I would cook the fish on a stick over a fire built near the water's edge. Without salt or butter, the soft white meat was accented only by a faint pungency of willow from the stick it was skewered on.

Before the magic of creek culture was lost to a growing boy, it was transformed. The south fork of Little Campbell Creek never relinquished its charm; it just passed it on to other waters. My uncle staked a homestead on Fish Creek north of Anchorage. The creek had more water, bigger trout, and salmon. Armed with a fly rod and my dad's old wickerwork

5

creel, I spent many weekends in a trance. I would let a dry fly drift with the current past riffles, over the swelling watery curve of a submerged log, onto the surface of a pool. The feathery imitation of a mosquito would disappear into the water when a fish struck, with a sound like a skipping stone thrown off angle. *Bluuop*. That sound was followed by a small fury, the leader slicing back and forth through the water, the tip of the pole nodding its approval, glimpses of color flashing ever slower until a rainbow eased into my waiting hand.

Occasionally I would fish upstream near the Mahoneys', my uncle's nearest neighbors, but it was mostly the downstream waters that I haunted. As I eased up to each familiar eddy, undercut bank, or rock, I replayed the scene of the last fish I'd caught at that spot. I was always hoping for a bigger one. Hours passed with only a handful of sounds: the gentle boil of water forming itself around my rubber boots, the faint whistle of flyline arcing past my head, my own breath.

Much as one stream's flow is diffused by others on its way to becoming a river, my interest in fishing diminished. Girls entered the picture, though not nearly as often as I would have liked. Music, cars, and climbing shared the spotlight with tackle and tippets. When I did fish, I chose secluded spots. On the banks of Moose River, just upstream from its confluence with the Kenai, was a quiet place shared with family and friends. But each year more boot tracks marked the soft shoreline and more brush was hacked from the water's edge. Even in the early morning hours it became hard to escape the sound of heavy lures plunking the water like persistent hail.

My friend Jim told me about the sockeye salmon run at the Russian River. There were a lot of people, but even more fish, he assured me. It was easy to catch your limit. When I saw the numerous cars and trucks parked across from the river's mouth, I drove on. The joy of fishing was lost to me with the crowd.

When I was in my early twenties, I bought five wooded acres on the lower Kenai Peninsula. With the help of family and friends I built a small cabin. I worked a few short-term construction jobs and explored the area, trying to decide if I should stay beyond autumn. The chinook salmon run in the Anchor River, a short drive from my cabin, was well known and popular. Fishermen would stand along some stretches of the river's bank, not elbow to elbow exactly, but more like pines in a Christmas tree farm.

For a while I held to my conviction to avoid such places. As I became comfortable with the area and entertained thoughts of staying permanently, I became more proprietary. It was my new neighborhood and the fish that swam in its streams were equally mine. Maybe I could learn to endure the crowds. Acceptance and maybe enjoyment too, could be achieved through practice, I thought.

Early one morning, I loaded my hip boots and rod into my Volkswagon van and drove to the Anchor. Dampness intertwined with the dawn as I shuffled to the river. I watched the queue of fishermen cast their lines slightly upstream, each reel spinning furiously as the current swept the lures down. Cast. Retrieve. Cast. Retrieve. No smiles. No laughter. Just grim determination.

For ten minutes or more I watched, caught up in the rhythm of flowing water and singing lines before I turned around and walked back to the parking area. As I set my rod inside the van I thought how ridiculous it was for me to leave without even getting my line wet. Returning to the water's edge, I located the widest opening between two fishermen and walked in the river up to my knees. My lure fell obediently, exactly where I intended. I reeled in and the clear line dripped water until the spool was full. One cast. I left and never went back.

I think of how human interests developed early in life often stay with us. Adult passions seem like a modified version of a child's delight. The boy from my neighborhood who pushed toy trucks around now operates heavy equipment for a living. The other friend, who mixed and matched model cars and ships, is an engineer. My diverse occupations included outdoor work as much as possible. I felt most at home when guiding in the backcountry or hauling crab pots from saltwater bays. The pull of streams never diminished; coming across even the slightest trickle in forested country still elicits in me that childhood sense of abandon.

These days, I subsistence fish for salmon with a net and put set lines out for burbot. Just a few times each year, usually in the spring when the ice is newly gone, or in early winter before the lake caps over, I'll pick up a fishing pole and walk to the water's edge. Standing alone, I'll cast into the clear water. Ice often clogs the rod's tip after a few minutes. I taste the glacial bite of line and steel as I place the tip in my mouth to melt away the obstruction. Gloves keep my fingertips from turning white while I cast and vow to stop at some number—ten or twenty—that I snatch out of the air to suit my mood. But I seldom stop at my intended goal. I continue on, in a timeless present, savoring one last cast.

2

Hats Off to Hal

I first met Hal in the third grade. My family had just moved from Spenard to our homesite on O'Malley Road above Anchorage, and I was fretting my way through the first week at a new school. During recess I wandered off to the far end of the hockey rink to avoid contact with the other kids, when I found myself on the turf of the playground bullies. They surrounded me, and the tallest of the three shoved me backwards. "What are you doing here?" he asked threateningly. Before I had time to reply, two other boys approached. Both wore crew cuts and gray sweatshirts. The larger of the two faced the bullies. "What's going on? You leave him alone." With this gesture Hal won my trust, a trust that hasn't faltered for the forty-five years we've been friends.

Flying in Alaska was almost a birthright for Hal; for twenty-three years his father was a valued pilot for Reeve Aleutian Airways. You didn't fly for crusty old Bob Reeve unless you were darn good, and that mix of common sense, courage, and caution it takes to be a good pilot was passed on from father to son.

That isn't to say that flying with Hal wasn't interesting and sometimes a lot of work. Take, for example, the time we had to snowshoe a runway in waist-deep snow.

Hal had offered to fly our mutual friend Jeff and me out to see Jeff's newly purchased lodge, nestled in a remote valley of the Chugach Mountains. We threw our gear in the back of the ski-equipped Cessna and headed east. The cool, stable February air embraced us as we lifted off the snow-covered ice of Fuller Lake in the Matanuska Valley. After passing Tazlina Lake, I pulled out the sectional and tracked our course with my finger. This was new country for all of us and we were savoring every moment.

Before long, a line of buildings appeared with snow piled high on the roofs. After circling several times, Hal picked a nearby clearing to land. Touchdown was smooth, but when he turned to taxi back into his tracks, the Cessna settled deeply and refused to budge. After Hal shut the engine down, we lashed on our snowshoes and packed a ramp and a small parking area.

Once the plane was sitting on the square of packed snow, its engine cover firmly in place, we plodded off toward the lodge. Jeff was visibly relieved to find he had purchased more than just photographs. He actually owned buildings, sturdy enough to still be standing under a heavy weight of snow. We shoveled as much from the roofs as time allowed, then dutifully returned to pack out a runway.

Side-by-side, we started out engaged in good-natured bantering but soon fell silent. I lost my sense of time but gained, or at least refreshed, the knowledge that deep snow and snowshoes equal sweat. Lift, plod, lift, plod—back and forth, down eight hundred feet of runway. Our progress seemed more vertical than horizontal, and the exertion made us shed our down parkas and heavy mittens. Finally Hal stopped, scrutinized our work, and announced, "That should be good enough." I teased him about the last time I had helped him pack out a runway at Twin Lakes, roughly fifty miles to the northwest. After hours of labor, the skis had caught on a small ridge of snow within the first thirty feet, sending us into deep powder and resulting in a protracted takeoff. I was determined not to let the same thing happen. As Hal and Jeff readied the airplane I continued widening the first one-third of the airstrip, until I was sure there was no way Hal would be making a similar performance.

We climbed in and Hal advanced the throttle. The plane surged forward and promptly plunged into unpacked snow. Despite our extra effort, the runway was still too narrow. Through the din of the laboring engine and the blur of flying snow, I watched us plow ahead. In the next instant, a beaver dam on the far end of the clearing loomed in front of us. "Damn," I thought, "That thing sure looks big." From my backseat perspective our momentum seemed too slow for the airplane to lift off. As I leaned forward trying to get a better view, I expected at any moment to hear the throttle cut, but we soon broke out of the snow and soared over the dam with plenty of room to spare.

Usually, when delegated to the back seat, I am a bit envious of the view up front. Of course there are times when that view isn't so great either. In the late 1970s, when the Iditarod Trail Sled Dog Race was still in its infancy, before the smoke-filled summer of the Farewell Burn, Hal flew his Taylorcraft from Anchorage to Farewell Lake Lodge where I was working as a caretaker. It was just before Christmas and Hal had offered me a ride back to town to visit family and purchase supplies I would need for the remainder of the winter. We spent one day pulling traps and securing camp for my temporary absence. Above all, trapping was an excuse for me to traipse through the wilderness observing animal sign. I snowshoed a lot, studied spoor, and caught very little—my one lynx lay on top of the woodpile in the freezing air. I hoped to skin it in the comfort of my Dad's heated garage when I got to town.

Hal and I spent the evening swapping stories and finishing off a huge batch of moose ribs. It wasn't until early the next morning, carrying the lynx to the airplane, that I realized my mistake. The animal's legs stuck straight out from the body and were so rigid I couldn't move them. Even in such a cumbersome position a lynx is not a large animal, but the Taylorcraft is not a big airplane, especially in the winter when the diminutive baggage area is already near capacity with gear—sleeping bags, wing covers, engine cover, and the like—a flying stuff sack full of nylon and down. But for a guy whose dad once flew Annabelle, Alaska's first elephant, to Nome in a DC-6, this wasn't a problem. Hal got the lynx inside the door, but after attempting several positions he still couldn't fit the frozen package fully inside the baggage compartment. The huge feet stuck high over the passenger seat, and as I slipped in and leaned back it was like putting on a fur headset—with claws. At least Hal could see well, and I figured that was all that really mattered.

Slowly gaining altitude, we worked our way up the south fork of the Kuskokwim River, turned east at Denny Creek, and entered Goodman Pass. My drifting thoughts suddenly snapped to attention when the engine began to sputter, but Hal's application of carburetor heat seemed to smooth things out, and after a couple of precautionary circles we continued through the pass. We were a good way down Ptarmigan Valley when the engine started acting up again. The tickle in the throat of the carburetor we had heard earlier was nothing compared to this chronic cough. It was followed by one of the most unnerving sounds a pilot can hear—silence.

I didn't say anything, but I sat bolt upright and took a deep breath. Hal asked me if I could tell which way the wind was blowing on the surface. I turned my head to the left—lynx paw. To the right—lynx paw. Then I leaned forward and was able to make out several stands of black spruce interspersed with small clearings. The tops of the trees bobbed gently, but despite my concentration I could see no wind pattern. Such a simple request, yet I sat as silent as the engine, unable to help our cause. I fixated on the largest of the tiny openings between the trees, hoping it was only our altitude that made the slot look so small. Hal said he thought we could make it to Puntilla Lake.

The mere mention of the choicest landing spot for miles provided an instant balm for my apprehension. Hal was attentive but composed as we glided down in gentle circles, even as several attempts to restart the engine proved fruitless. The skis touched the snow and we slid to a smooth stop. I teased Hal with the truth: "That was a better landing than when you *have* power!"

Hal surmised the most likely cause of our problem: carburetor icing. In simple terms it occurs when moisture in the air forms ice on the throat of the carburetor, choking off the intake of oxygen. The trouble was, as soon as the aircraft stopped moving, any ice that had formed would quickly melt due to heat radiating from the engine, leaving no evidence to confirm the diagnosis. We checked the fuel tanks and engine for signs of any other possible cause, but found none.

The mountain rising from the west shore of the lake slowly

washed from white to slate. Like the sun, we decided to continue our travels through the sky the following morning.

Smoke angled away in a thin column from the roof of Rainy Pass Lodge, the only dwelling on the lake. We snowshoed to the lodge. The caretakers welcomed us inside, handed us bowls of hot moose stew, and offered use of the radiotelephone. We had simply intended to let them know who was parked and camped nearby as a courtesy, but we found their hospitality too enticing.

The glow of embers shone through the open draft of the barrel stove as Hal and I moved toward its warmth. "I can have someone come out to get you tomorrow if you don't want to get back in my airplane," he said. The thought had not occurred to me, and I felt a pang of disloyalty to even consider the idea. Bolstered by the intoxication and security of warmth, food, and friendship I answered, "If you're willing to try, I can't let you go alone."

In the crisp air of morning we lifted off the snowy surface headed for Anchorage. Nervously I listened for a change in the sound of the engine, but it purred like a contented kitten all the way to Lake Hood. Crawling into the passenger seat had been more unsettling than I'd imagined, but I had no way of knowing the most difficult time I would have getting into an airplane with Hal would come years later. A different airplane, another lake.

Caught up in one of Alaska's many land rushes, Hal and I spent early January one winter tent-camping in temperatures down to minus thirty-seven degrees, claiming land on a lake northeast of Anchorage. Hal's wife and my father had quickly surveyed the situation and concluded that the job of clearing lines around our forty-acre parcels would take much longer than anticipated. They left us with best wishes and a bow saw.

Hal and I cut branches and trees, paced, measured, and plotted our way through the six hours of light available each day. Finally, our last corner post was set and our bearings all double-checked. We only needed to transfer our notes and computations onto the lengthy state application forms, but the idea of doing so in such cold temperatures convinced us to spend our last night in nearby Eureka.

Hal landed his Stinson on the snow-covered lake next to the roadhouse. We spent the night sitting red-faced on the high-backed benches of the café booth, listening to the sizzle of burgers frying on the grill. White frost lined the bottom of the windows, underscoring our view of the cold world outside. I wondered if our sinews were beginning to soften, but Hal assured me we were merely getting smarter. We had a good laugh and a warm night.

We started the next day by preheating our own engines with breakfast at the café. Then, with plenty of coffee in our tanks, we began the winter ritual of refueling and preheating the airplane. Loaded, warmed-up, and ready to head to town, we rocked the plane, making sure the skis weren't sticking. We climbed in.

The 190-horsepower engine roared, but no matter how much Hal tried bouncing the tail and working the rudder, the plane wouldn't budge. Skis often refreeze to the surface during the start-up procedure, so I crawled out into knee-deep snow and pushed on the wing strut while Hal advanced the throttle. The airplane started to slide.

Hal shouted, "I'll pick you up the next time around."

I watched as he taxied around the perimeter of the lake,

thinking, erroneously, that when he completed the circle he would stop to let me climb aboard.

As he pulled even with me he yelled, "Try to hop in!"

I found out quickly why Carl Lewis never competed in shoepacks, long johns, and wool pants. To liken the labored floundering of my appendages to a sprint was, in generous terms, absurd.

Although Hal was barely moving, he was pulling away from me at a steady rate. Winded, I halted abruptly and watched the airplane begin another lap of the lake. Hiking up my sagging long johns, I thought, "Timing. It's all a matter of timing."

I crouched down, kicked together some makeshift starting blocks in the snow, and began coaching myself.

Ready? No, Not yet.

Hal turned the final corner.

Three, two, one. Go!

Loping along, I began building momentum, saving my kick for the moment when I was even with the rear of the ski.

Now!

I'm gaining ground . . . I can do this.

Left boot on the tail of the ski, right hand on the strut—I pulled myself onto the victory platform. Then, whoosh! The prop wash blew off my fur hat. A quick glance to Hal and I bailed off back into the snow.

Panting heavily, I tied the leather laces of my hat tightly under my chin. Now I had the technique refined and the practice runs out of the way. Soon I would be sitting aboard next to my friend and—once I caught my breath—looking forward to the next adventure. Whether it required cleats, shoepacks, or bunny boots, I knew I would be ready to lace them up.

Burn

On a hot afternoon in July 1979, a pilot landed his airplane at Stan Frost's private airstrip at Farewell Lake where I was working for the summer. Keeping with proper bush etiquette, he handed me two plastic five-gallon containers full of gas, replacing what he had borrowed the previous summer. He relieved himself in the nearby bushes, then ambled down to the lodge to chat. I found a couple of empty metal cans and a funnel and started to transfer the gasoline so he could return to town with his containers.

No one had told me that gasoline builds up a charge as it flows, and the faster it is poured, the more charge is generated. No one had yet shown me how to equalize the static electricity buildup either by connecting the containers with a wire or keeping them in continuous contact with each other. I just poured the liquid rapidly from the first container, leaving several inches between its nozzle and the funnel.

There was the faintest sound of a snap, like a small, brittle pencil breaking in the next room. Then I was holding flames. Without thinking, I flung the container away from me. Spreading flames in its wake, it rolled up against a partially full fifty-five gallon drum of gasoline. The fire danced effortlessly up the hose of the hand pump that was mounted on the drum. I tried futilely to kick up dirt to smother it, but the ground was rock hard and all I produced was dust.

Next to the partially filled drum stood a full one, and twenty feet away, a three-hundred gallon tank of diesel fuel with propane tanks nearby. Having watched enough Hollywood movies and television shows to know a massive explosion was imminent, I ran a short distance away and dove in behind a dirt bank.

Nothing exploded, but when I peered over the edge to look, flames were still raking the pump's hose and black smoke snaked up in tiny wisps from the melting rubber. I dashed to the shop to search for an extinguisher and madly cranked the handle on the old military field phone to call the lodge for help, imagining buildings reduced to ashes, flames crowning spruce, and summer clouds orange-red in reflection of unnatural heat. The swiftness of that spark matched the speed of my surging emotions: helplessness and panic.

Every summer, wildfires rage and smolder across Alaska, most started by lightning strikes, but every year some are started by people—usually the careless or uninformed. When the genesis for wildfires is natural it somehow seems more acceptable, even if it takes several human generations for the country to fully rebound. When folks are careless, the resulting flames seem malicious, the smoke more acrid. My first impulse is to pass harsh judgment on the guilty person: "Why didn't he dump more water on the coals? Why was he burning brush or setting off fireworks when the country was dry or it was windy?"

Although basic rules for fire prevention can be taught, laziness or arrogance sometimes overrides our actions and the preventable happens. But sometimes a new lesson is sudden. On that sweltering summer day, I learned something about static electricity that was a far cry from childhood novelties, such as rubbing a balloon on my head so it would stick to the ceiling, or producing visible sparks on my fingertips after shuffling across the carpet in winter.

It was a humbling experience. Had the fire erupted and the surrounding vegetation caught, a wildfire could easily have ensued. For the first time, I felt the weight of responsibility for the immensity of the accompanying loss, and sympathetic to the inadvertent perpetrators of such destruction. I had seen a wildfire's seething handiwork two summers earlier, in the first year I worked for Stan.

Blue-gray air tinted the downstream valley, as if the mountains had stepped into their own shadows. I paid little attention, thinking the gunmetal tone could be blinked into clarity, like the first vision of morning after a night of heavy sleep. I turned back to the pile of firewood I had been working on and gripped my axe. When I looked again to the north, the slopes of the Terra Cotta and Teocalli Mountains that rose up from the Hartman River had darkened to a premature dusk. Ridges, gullies, rock faces, and green slopes lost their edges beneath a mask of smoke.

Stan had dropped me off near the big bend in the Hartman at Tundra Camp, so named because it had easy access to the dwarf shrub, moss, and lichen-covered areas above timberline. Instructions to prepare the place for the approaching hunting season had, until now, focused my attention. I had scraped parka squirrel poop from dishes, table, and floor and ushered the dark nuggets out the door with a short-handled broom. I had gathered the fractured and wind-whipped remains of plastic sheeting from a wide swath around the camp. A bear's entrance through a shuttered window had scattered splinters of wood and broken glass that were now bagged and waiting to be flown out with the other trash. The lantern and gas stove were in good running condition, with new mantles and oil for the pump leathers. With bow saw and axe I worked on the last item on my list, bucking up the woodpile.

Not one airplane had rumbled a distant greeting since Stan's Super Cub faded from sight nearly a week ago. I had no radio for communication, only Stan's word that he would return in a couple of days. I had been enjoying the solitude, working at my own pace, and above all, the quiet. It was only the second time in the two months I had worked for Stan that I'd ventured away from the lodge by myself. I was twenty-three years old and more alone than I had ever been in my life.

Before cleaning up Tundra camp, I had mucked out another one on the Jones River. While I was on the Jones, Stan flew in with a few bags of groceries one day and casually mentioned he'd spotted a forest fire almost five acres in size on a flight from McGrath back to his lodge. He'd called the Flight Service Station to report the blaze.

I hadn't given it much thought, perhaps because my experience with uncontrolled fire was limited. Once, while on a canoe trip through a popular chain of lakes on the Kenai Peninsula, three teenage friends and I spotted smoke rising from a distant shore. Paddling close to chat with the campers, we were surprised to find no one nearby. Smoke emanated not only from a fire pit, but also from the hollows at the bases of several trees and numerous mossy hummocks.

The area was almost an acre in size. A pungent odor permeated the scene and smoke hung like a smudge beneath the forest's canopy.

We emptied our cooler of its contents and grabbed several cooking pots. Load after load of water we hauled from the lake and poured onto the steaming ground. Spots of warm orange glow between interlocking roots hissed and steamed with every cooler load. We doused until our muscles ached. The day slipped away and evening arrived as the last wisp of smoke dissipated. A decision was made to spend the night so we could make sure the fire had been extinguished. The following morning, we paddled on.

Another time, I was in Anchorage when an urban wildfire threatened a high school, and a friend told me the Bureau of Land Management (BLM) was hiring. I was given a job and told to report to the field office set up at the school. I thought I would be on the front line fighting back flames, but the supervisor handed me a hard hat and told me to stand at the entrance to the school. For two days I was a security guard keeping the public at bay. From where I stood, feeling feckless and stiff under a plastic hard hat, I watched airplanes dumping retardant while smoke billowed over the treetops. The fire was controlled quickly and I was relieved of my duties.

Remembering Stan's report, I looked again at the smoke and felt the first stirrings of alarm. Already Stan was late picking me up. Could that small fire he'd seen have grown to a monster and overtaken the lodge? Was it racing up fifty-some miles of river valley into the heart of the Alaska Range where I stood? I searched through the gauzy air with my binoculars for a sign of flame. Nothing. I told myself everything was fine back at the lodge, but the smoky air had a somber presence. For the first time, being alone in the wild felt more like abandonment than freedom.

What would I do if flames appeared five miles away and an hour later half that distance? I had no map to plan an escape route. I could load my pack with food, climb the mountain behind camp, and wait. I could follow the riverbed farther into the mountains, or at the last moment I could rush out to the largest gravel island in the river and hunker down. Maybe the motion and coolness of the river would form a low-slung column of smoke-free air to breathe.

Several times that evening I walked out from the cabin to stand at the river's edge. The mountainous skyline was indistinct, floating in the murky air above the valley. A mixture of jingling stones and a constant, lightsome splash, chimed up from the water rushing past. Here and there, handfuls of gravel sloughed from the bank into the river.

When I awoke the next morning the sky was clear. The wind had reversed itself and wiped clean all trace of smoke. The previous day's darkness and concerns seemed like a brief illusion. I sang to myself throughout the day and into the evening hours as I worked.

The following day I heard the purring of an airplane long before I spotted Stan's white and red Piper flying up the valley. Making a low pass, he banked steeply and landed on the patch of gravel in front of camp. He taxied up almost to the front door of the tent cabin, shut the engine down, and swung himself out of the cockpit. "Grab your gear, Steve, I need you back at the lodge," he said.

As we loaded my sleeping bag, rifle, and trash into the airplane, Stan told me that the wildfire was out of control: it had recently jumped several fire lines and was within four miles of the lodge. He said that helicopters and airplanes were working along with crews on the ground, and personnel from the BLM had talked to him about evacuation plans.

We flew low on our way down the valley. As we approached the Rohn River I noticed the sky's smoky tinge and smelled burning wood. Visibility decreased. Abreast of Egypt Mountain we began hugging the west bank of the braided south Fork of the Kuskokwim River. Looking over Stan's shoulder through the windshield, I saw a wall of gray. Only by gazing forward and down like a hawk could I make out any details. Gravel bars, willows, and piles of driftwood streaked by.

I thought conditions must have deteriorated a great deal since Stan began his flight to retrieve me, because I couldn't imagine a pilot taking off with such poor visibility. Stan reduced our speed by backing off on the throttle and pulling half flaps, much as a driver would slow down when entering fog on a highway. I expected him to turn around any moment and fly upriver to clearer air, but he kept going.

Brief images of willow, spruce, alder, birch, and poplar montaged below us in rapid intervals of variegated green. Tin Creek flashed by as a thin, silver ribbon. The collapsing log buildings and dog barns of the abandoned Iditarod roadhouse we called Frenchy Joe's appeared for a second then were gone. We turned left and flew up a marsh. To each side of the spring-fed lowland rose trees that were higher than our altitude. Somewhere in the grayness ahead was a hill. Stan pushed the throttle forward, and as we climbed the marsh dropped away. Under full power we cleared the treetops, then Stan cut the throttle, turned right, and his narrow dirt airstrip appeared below us.

Much had happened while I'd been at the outer camps. The fire in just the first four days grew from five acres to an estimated 55,000 acres. Manpower swelled from an initial eighteen to 172. Air support increased to include three helicopters and one airplane.

It was a dry year in an arid part of Alaska, and on August 10 the fire had exploded. Temperatures reached eighty degrees Fahrenheit with a relative humidity of only twenty-six percent. Towering columns of smoke shot gases 145 feet into the sky, making reconnaissance difficult. Flames knocked down by direct attack sprung back to life almost immediately with the help of winds that exceeded twenty miles per hour. A crew protecting their own spike camp was forced to retreat, and their camp was lost to flames.

The smoke at the lodge was thick. Across the lawn, the cache, the root cellar, and the old cabin that served as a bunkhouse seemed to float free of one another. I had thought of the structures as a rustic trio, but in the murk nothing appeared connected. Gasoline water pumps sat on the mown grass. Short hoses stretched from them down into the lake and long ones snaked their way up the slopes toward surrounding buildings. Helicopters flew by unseen, at times sounding close enough to touch.

Stan's wife, Marta, and his daughter, Cathy, told me about the amphibious airplane, a PBY Catalina that had been busy working the fire. It repeatedly descended directly over the lodge and settled on the surface of the lake. While doing high-speed taxis, the pilot of the Catalina scooped water into a belly tank then powered his way back into the air to dump the load on the fire. On one pass the airplane caught a wing tip in the water and spun sideways in a partial water loop.

The pilot shut down both engines and someone crawled out on the wings, roaming up and down, inspecting for damage. The pilot eventually restarted the engines and took off. Marta and Cathy hadn't seen the airplane return, and they assumed it was no longer airworthy.

I wasn't needed in the heroic way I'd imagined: a soot-faced fighter of flames snuffing out hotspots with a Pulaski, or felling trees in rapid succession to clear a firebreak. All of Stan's guides were in outer camps with clients, and someone had to do the chores. I filled wood boxes, replaced empty propane tanks with full ones, butchered meat, and salted hides while the fire raged on.

I soon learned to tell which way the wind was blowing without feeling a breeze on my face or looking at any of the direction indicators: the Alaska Flag hanging near the lodge entrance, the windsock at the airstrip, or the surface of the lake. If wind was funneling out of the mountains from the southeast, the air would clear enough to reveal trees, buildings, and dirt trails. Any movement of air from a northerly direction blurred objects from the ground up in gradations of increasing density, like a charcoal sketch. Along with a mask of gray was the pungent smell of a fire whose appetite stretched beyond trees to gobble up grasses, mosses, voles, and squirrels, and burn six inches into the ground.

As the days progressed, temperatures rose to ninety degrees Fahrenheit and the humidity dropped to twenty percent. Vegetation was tinder dry. The trails that networked around Stan's property were like baked clay. The sun had transformed into a huge orange-red ball, and swirling winds brought waves of heat in from odd angles.

Not a man lacking self-confidence, Stan flew to the BLM field office to talk with the person in charge. Stan believed the first crews had missed an opportunity to quell the fire early on. He ended up nose to nose with the fire boss in a heated discussion regarding wind direction and lack of action. Cathy, who had tagged along, stepped between them to diffuse the situation.

In three weeks time the fire had burned 255,000 acres, seen five different fire bosses in charge, and showed no signs of abating. Five bulldozers were out on the land dropping their blades, making long-lasting scars that often did little to slow the fire's advance. At one point when the fire, assisted by a north wind, was moving rapidly toward the lodge, Stan was told not to worry: the BLM would bring in fifty people to spray the buildings down with water and clear surrounding trees to save the lodge. Stan told them if they were going to let the country go up in flames, they may as well let the lodge go too. He wanted to know, "What the hell good is a hunting lodge sitting in the middle of a burn?"

Stan was tired of what he called, unequivocally, "bullshit." He flew to the nearest telephone at Farewell Station and called John Dingell, a senator from Michigan whom he had met when the senator was on a tour of Alaska. Stan urged him to help in any way he could. He made a similar call to Jay Hammond, then governor of Alaska. Hammond was not only a fellow big-game guide, but he had briefly owned the property at the south end of Farewell Lake where Stan's lodge stood. Shortly after the phone calls, a Class I overhead team from the contiguous United States arrived on the fire.

More acreage was lost and the personnel assigned to the fire rose to 361 souls. Experienced crews from Hooper Bay,

Stebbins, Unalakleet, and many other villages labored wherever they were needed. The equipment dedicated to the fire was impressive: helicopters, airplanes, bulldozers, and ATVs topped the list. But for all the noble efforts to fight the fire, it was the change of season that probably had the most profound effect.

During the first week of September, temperatures lowered and humidity inched upward. The blaze began moving slowly for the first time in weeks, although it still burned hot in pockets of spruce. The second week of the month ushered in a stretch of cool and wet weather that took the heat out of the fire.

At 8 p.m. on September 9, 1977 the fire was finally contained. Four days later it was declared controlled, and demobilization plans were put into effect. Crews and aircraft were released. Cargo airplanes back hauled bulldozers and thousands of pounds of gear to Anchorage. On September 24 the last four members of the BLM team left behind 361,600 burned acres, the largest wildfire of the year.

The lightning-caused fire was officially called the Bear Creek fire, for its point of origin. But the blaze is better known as the Farewell Burn, due to the fire's proximity to the nearby mountain, lake, and landing strip that share the name.

When I first discovered the abandoned camp shortly after the fire, I wanted to tear it down. It was ugly, and tainted the view of a pristine spot that lay not far beyond the southern reach of the burn. The lopsided, spindly structure marked a temporary camp used by firefighters. I never took the time to dismantle it. For years the frame held, and served as a reminder of the massive amount of human effort put into fighting the fire. I never found out which crew lashed together those spruce poles, but I started referring to the small lake nearby as the BLM pond. That frame slowly collapsed back into the tundra over the course of a decade.

Charring a chunk of Stan's neighborhood almost the size of Rhode Island, the fire affected his business for years. Stan said that fire lines and cat trails altered moose movements, especially during the rut. I took Stan's word for it; my time in the area before the fire was too brief for me to judge. Biologists claim that although fire can kill animals, the threat to wildlife populations is minor. Most negative effects from a wildfire are short term, while the positive effects due to high-quality habitat regeneration are great. In the midst of such devastation, it's hard to see that.

Ten years later I hiked into the burn to look around. Somewhere between Bear Creek and the south fork of the Kuskokwim, I climbed one of the highest hills. The top of the small knoll was an inert gray. A few charred and limbless spruce pointed to the sky, while other, fallen trees were broken and crosshatched obstacles to walking. Ash was inches thick in the earth where I dug down with the toe of my boot. Nowhere on that hill could I find a sign of new growth. Located in one of the driest parts of the state, the area's sparse rainfall and snowmelt moves minerals back into the soil with painstaking slowness.

I dropped down the backside of the knoll feeling estranged from any living thing. But there, in the lowest parts of the cut below, pale-green mosses maintained the spongy feel of walking on a worn-out mattress. A few blades of grass protruded in small clumps. Nothing was vivid, just a gentle trace of color and feeling of resiliency beneath my feet.

Here were two faces of the wildfire's aftermath only strides apart: the fierce burning of one area adjacent to the singeing of another. I could envision the mosaic of varied habitats for plants and animals that would someday flourish. But it would take time, a lot of time. I walked the miles back to the lodge, traces of ash falling from my boots.

4

Standing on a Heart

There are places on the trail that hold ghosts. Places that haunt and beckon us. Trees or fields, ridges or rocks that trap us. Forever dust and deadfall, the slow snake of the path curves and shrinks into nothingness.

For me, one such place lies where an old jeep trail, linking Farewell Lake to Farewell Station, passes near the west end of John Lake. As small patches of boreal forest go, it is unremarkable. If you are walking with the morning sun at your back, something eases you down the rutted track. A gentle downhill and the pull of the earth make you believe you could walk on endlessly. Dwarf birch gives way to tall grass as you approach the stand of white spruce hunched at the bottom. To the right the conifers are larger than most in the area. A deep game trail winds under their boughs, up from the edge of the lake. You can't see the water, or how the lake wraps itself, moatlike, around three sides of a steep ridge. But you can feel it. I have passed this place in the boot-sole-sink of spring, known the dust and mosquito buzz of midsummer, the crisp flirtation of autumn, and the cold that follows.

In my history here, there is a sadness too. Even the red squirrel's bark loses its edge as the sound weaves down through the boughs, more a lament than a scolding. Spruce-cone detritus forms random, soggy piles beneath the tallest trees. There is a graying at the edges of things: the gnarled roots of an alder, a withered bolete abandoned on a branch, the shape of my hand.

It was the late 1970s and I was doing what young, single, wilderness lodge caretakers did in Alaska during the winter: trap. There was a rhythm to most days that I came to expect and love: each morning's first sensation of cool air on my face; looking up at the swirl of metal springs on the underbelly of the upper bunk; a glance to the cassette deck mounted on a wooden shelf, surrounded by the little boxes containing my favorite tunes, all within arm's reach; my left shoulder leaning against the chestnut-hued log wall. And, as if I were the one to introduce sound and smell to the world each morning, the creaking of the plank floor as I walked over to the barrel stove, the crackle of dried spruce, followed by the perk and aroma of coffee. In many ways the setting was idyllic. It seemed I was finally leading the life that I had dreamed about for so many years.

What I knew about trapping came from reading and from casual comments from outdoorsmen I'd met. My father, an avid hunter and fisherman, didn't want any part of trapping. He'd grown up on a farm in Wisconsin, and through most of his teenage years his parents raised mink. When his brothers left home to serve in the military during World War II, he was the one who fed the mink and cleaned their cages. He broke their necks and skinned them. He smelled the strong odor of confinement and felt the pain of their teeth sinking through leather gloves into the meat of his fingers.

Under the hiss and brightness of a gas lantern I studied my dog-eared trapping manual. In the field, I studied harder. Much of what I read about animal behavior turned out to be true.

Beneath the protecting branches of a spruce tree, I spiked a stout, dry, seven-foot pole that ran diagonally from the ground and protruded eighteen inches past the tree. Called a pole set, it is a favorite of trappers working marten country. The trap and bait are placed on the upper end, and the marten, a tree climber, ascends the pole to reach the bait and consequently steps into the trap. The trap is secured lightly to the pole with a string, wire, or bent nail, and as the animal struggles the trap drops off and swings clear, taking the marten with it. In cold weather the animals freeze quickly, usually in a few hours. That is how I had always found them. Dead and frozen.

But a Chinook wind had warmed the December air above freezing. There was no need to stoke the barrel stove that morning to ensure a warm cabin upon my return. The strap-hinged, cotton batten-chinked door latched easily. Outside, my snowshoes rested on the brow tines of a huge set of moose antlers spiked to the front wall. I wouldn't need the webbed, wooden frames on the hard-packed trail. I shouldered my pack and began walking.

Within the first thirty minutes I passed two sets with nothing in them, but ahead there was movement. Beneath the pole, a marten hung inches from the ground, There was a minklike grace to its form. Stretched out, the animal looked sleeker than the ones I had seen peering down from the branches of black spruce, their soft, round ears framing teddy bear faces. The jaws of the Victor No. 1 single-spring held one front paw, its fine, ivory white claws emerging from the plush, brown fur. I unbuckled the belt of my pack, shoulder-dipped and arm-tucked my way out from under the straps.

This was supposed to be my moment, a chance to confirm

my membership in the fraternal order of mountain men, an opportunity to collect a token of manhood and some tangible proof that my time had not been wasted. Justification of existence on a primal level. But there was no thrill or sense of accomplishment, just a nagging pressure at my temples and a tightness in my chest.

The marten's efforts to escape came in waves: it was an amateur gymnast on the rings, struggling to perfect a new move, then swinging to rest. I had read that a sharp blow with a stick across the nose would stun a small animal and it would die quickly once you stood on its chest. The kicking and squirming of the marten intensified when I approached it with my walking stick half-cocked. The constant motion, the twirling of the furry mobile into new positions, made me check the first swing and the second. Finally, I choked up on my surrogate club for more speed and accuracy and rapped the marten in the face.

Whether the blow was off-angle or merely not hard enough, I don't know. The trap chain that was wired to the pole slipped several inches, and the animal's hind feet touched the ground. It lunged at me, jerking against the steel jaws that held its paw. I jumped back. My only recourse was to flail away with my stick like a man snuffing out a burning bush, until the marten lay there, stunned and twitching. I stepped forward quickly, one foot on its chest.

There was a taste of iron in my mouth. *Please die; please just let me kill you.* I cursed the steep and messy learning curve. I reprimanded myself, thinking I should have secured the trap chain better, positioned it farther up the pole so there was less chance of the marten touching the ground. I thought of the far too many squirrels and gray jays that had perished before I learned ways to hide my traps. And still, even with increased experience, there were unwanted deaths, remnants of fur, feathers, and blood.

We can learn a lot from reading, but there is nothing like experience. And there is no chronometer sensitive enough to measure the length of certain moments. Like the time I knelt a dozen feet away from a trapped lynx, wiring a snare in the shape of a noose to the end of a long pole, and the only sound was the squeak of dry snow against my boots as I stood. Because a bullet hole will bring less money for the skin, because lynx die easily. Cat eyes upon me, the loop of wire slipped over the feline neck. Lift up, up, I told myself, and the full weight of its death was in my hands.

What I didn't learn from reading trapping manuals is that finding my place in the life and death cycles on which all natural systems depend would be hard. Courage to change comes in increments, in admitting the difference between killing for food and killing for fur. For a while I tried to bridge that gap by eating the flesh of muskrat, beaver, and lynx. But I was eating the meat because of a self-imposed obligation to minimize waste, not because I relished the flavor. Though my lack of culinary skill was a factor, I never got past the greasy, sweet taste. Even though I sold the fur, I couldn't shake the thought that these creatures should be more than a commodity.

I quit trapping. Years passed and I came to live on another lake in remote Alaska, surrounded by different mountains. A neighbor to the east fed and photographed the animals; another to the west trapped and skinned them. One winter when I watched the easy gait of a westbound wolf, my heart lifted, then, too quickly, settled. I never heard the shot, but the voice of my neighbor was clear as he boasted over the VHF radio how he never had to leave his cabin, just picked up his rifle and opened the window.

Later I passed by the crumpled carcass, misshapen and bird-picked on the ice. The cold I felt was bone-and-muscle-deep, and the ice I stood on was not the only thing that had buckled and fractured.

I continue to hunt and fish for food, but something has changed. Salmon and burbot are filleted closer to the bone. Grouse blood stains fingers that hold the bird a bit longer to feel its warmth, its softness. Its feathers, its feet, its weight are all a part of me, and I think of my parents, my wife, and my friends. As if joy were to the east and sadness to the west, I stand on a hillside exactly in between, feeling both.

The experts tell how to trap a marten. What they don't mention is if the snow is too soft or deep, the body of the marten beneath the foot settles away from the crushing pressure. That it is necessary to put even more weight on that leg to finish the job. They didn't tell me whether the beating was coming from under my foot or from my own chest. Or how someday I would sit next to my mother in the hospital waiting room while my father's guts were in the hands of a surgeon. How my mother's heart, for decades enlarged and beating irregularly, would feel as if it were in my own hands. I look out the window at the mountains and imagine a small creature held by steel jaws. I remember a tiny patch of earth just west of John Lake and how nobody told me, as I stood on that heart and stared straight ahead, that the pulse of the moment would last such a long time.

5

Crabbing

I fished the last king crab season in Kodiak waters. It was December of 1982. Hal, the captain and my longtime friend, made it clear we were unlikely to get rich. This was not the Bering Sea, where crewmembers could earn over $50,000 in a few months. The high price of $3.75 for each pound of live crab delivered to the docks would not compensate for the low harvest forecast. The Kodiak fishery had been going strong for twenty-four years in Alaska. By the time I got involved it was winding down. For me though, it was a new adventure and a chance to reconnect with a friend, so I eagerly signed on.

On deck in the biting winter air Hal methodically taught me the carrick bend, the knot that connected the long lengths of stiff poly line to one another. This interlocking twist and bend of line was easily untied even after heavy stress; the knot rode straight through the hydraulic pot puller without hanging up or popping out. Hal showed me how to chop frozen herring by hand with a steel spud, to stuff the slurry of oily ooze into perforated plastic bait jars. I slashed the flesh of the cod we used as hanging bait and through their heads drove ten-inch stainless steel hooks to suspend them above the two jars of chopped herring. Herring juices would leak out to attract crab from a long distance, while the cod gave them something to pick on, a crustacean's hors d'oeuvre of sorts.

We repaired torn web on the pots and replaced wooden

tunnel boards that gave crab entrance to the 6-foot-square, 3-foot-high steel frames. As my hair curled in the salt air I learned how to throw the lines so they would uncoil easily and not tangle, to grip the 400-pound steel pots with authority and respect. I found satisfaction in the physicality of the work.

On those rare occasions when a refracted blur of orange showed in the pot as it was pulled through the last fathom of water to the surface, there was excitement on deck. Each male was tested for the legal size of eight inches by measuring across the widest part of its spiked carapace. We tossed the small females back into the sea.

Our boat had the second highest catch of the fleet working out of Port Lions. We caught forty-eight crab, not per pot or per day, but the entire season.

Two years later, and for the next seven, I was back on the *Marci La Rae* in search of tanner crab. Tanners are sometimes sold as snow crab in the stores, a more exotic and more marketable name. I suppose I felt a special connection with this smaller cousin of the king, since opening day of the season was always scheduled on my birthday, in the middle of January. After our last pot was set that first day, I would drink a beer while Hal and fellow crewmember Scott sang Happy Birthday. Then I would pull out my guitar. We'd sing Crosby, Stills and Nash, Roger Miller, Neil Young, and Creedence Clearwater Revival, and talk about how the crab were dropping one by one into the pots.

For six seasons the three of us were a team. Hal was a seasoned fisherman with a cool head whose deft touch made things run smoothly. Scott loved adventure, put his back to everything he did and never complained. We didn't snort cocaine, as many fishermen did in those days; we had a beer with dinner. We read Robert Service aloud, trading favorites. Though none of us could carry a tune in a deck bucket there was a strong undercurrent of harmony.

Some nights we'd rendezvous with Hal's brother-in-law, Robbie. Captain of the *Windigo*, he talked of heydays in the 1970s, when kings were abundant. He said there were so many crab that sometimes, in order to create more space, the crew used deck brushes to push them down into the hold or tied an octopus near the top of the tank so the crab would shrink away from their natural enemy. They would deck load what wouldn't fit below and make a run to the canneries, orange bodies of the catch heaped in a squirming pile, legs protruding from the scuppers. During these stories, Robbie would get a look in his eyes, like a man dizzy from a blow to the head, and tell how the crab just crawled up over a ledge somewhere, way out in the depths of the ocean. It was endless, this wellspring, it was just a matter of finding where the crab had congregated. I thought the tale was intended to poke fun at greenhorn landlubbers, but he revisited the myth too often. Clearly, he believed that abundant equaled limitless.

Crab fishing has been called the most dangerous job in America, but that label refers mostly to fishing the Bering Sea, where men fight stronger winds and larger waves and work around the clock. Everything is greater for them: the risks and the potential for big bucks.

Yet we too worked in rough water with pots heavy enough to maim or kill. We handled sharp knives on a wet or icy deck and danced clear of lines that could pull us overboard in an instant. But because of my confidence in Hal and Scott, I seldom felt in jeopardy.

Sometimes in rough seas a pot lifted aboard swung in an unexpected arc. Scott and I stepped back from some, subdued others. There was a rhythm to our reactions, anticipation we shared without words. Hal, operating the hydraulics, arrested the particularly savage swings by lowering the pot momentarily back into the sea. If my feet slipped, Scott's sure grip on the steel cage prevented it from crashing down.

We began to make profits only after expenses had been met. As captain, Hal paid the insurance premium, but the cost of fuel, bait, and food was split among the three of us. There was no cutting cost on fuel or bait. Our food supply was different. Most years we shot a deer from the nearby coastline. At low tide, we dug steamer clams by flashlight on the beach near the Port Lions airport. We kept them in an onion sack suspended in the same tank of circulating seawater that held the catch. Occasionally a small halibut would swim into a pot and we returned only the fins and entrails to the sea. We even sampled octopus.

The crab averaged a little more than two and a half pounds each and we knew the price offered at the docks. It was simple to calculate how many keepers we needed to break even. That was why we kept fishing even after the numbers were reduced to a scattered few. We generally caught eighty percent of our total in the first week. The first years I fished, I thought there were undiscovered holes that we would find after the initial push was over. The pattern was remarkably the same, however; our average per pot dropped steadily after the first few days, then we scraped the bottom until the end. We were always one of the last boats fishing.

A part of me wanted to grant clemency to the few crab left. They deserved a long hiatus from the intrusion of our pots. But I said nothing. I didn't want Hal to think I was a quitter. Let the fisheries experts set the season, quota, and size limit, I thought. Let Hal decide when enough is enough.

Though we were fishing tanners, there were areas that also held Dungeness and king. Often the species would intermingle. When the $3/4$-inch poly line squeaked and made tiny popping sounds as it rode through the puller, we knew it as the song of a heavy pot. Heavy often meant female kings, since there weren't many males left and adults tend to segregate by sex. Hal turned several over to show me the thousands of embryos underneath their tail flap. A dull brown fungus covered the eggs. The cause was uncertain even to the biologists, but they suspected that it was a key factor in the kings' decline.

We kept some of the larger males to eat. We dropped the legs into a pot of boiling water on the galley stove and when time allowed, pulled them from the bubbling pot and stepped out on deck. Leaning against the rails for stability, we gorged ourselves on the thick tubes of succulent meat, salted to perfection by the clean ocean water. Juices flowed through our beards and down our chins and we never longed for butter or garlic.

Not all my experiences at sea were so pleasurable. Once, eleven days into my third tanner season, we faced twelve foot swells on a four-and-a-half-hour run from Port Lions to Kodiak. I braced myself against the galley counter, holding tighter as each wall of green water hurled itself at the front windows. It was understood that nobody went out on deck in conditions like this. If we needed to relieve ourselves, we stood at the edge of the doorway and did the job to the best of our abilities.

Loaded with almost 14,000 pounds of crab—ninety-five percent of the season's catch—the *Marci La Rae* cut slowly through the froth. Added to our physical discomfort was the nagging fear that the crab might not be deliverable. Somewhere in the past two days we'd spent the night too near a source of fresh water and unknowingly circulated it through the hold. When crab die without being immediately cooked or frozen, a cellular breakdown rapidly kicks in and their flesh becomes unpalatable.

When Hal noticed the listless crab, he made a quick diagnosis of the problem and headed for deep water. Hoping to revive them, he increased the pump speed, flushing saline through their systems. The crab did not respond. We weren't sure what the processors' guidelines were. How "alive" did the crab need to be? Hal's pale blue eyes flashed at his watch, the tachometer, and back to his watch.

When we finally approached the cannery, a radio check brought news that we were second in line, behind the *Ruff & Ready*. The wait would be several hours. As we filled our fuel and fresh water tanks, we pulled several crab from the hold. Their legs drooped from their bodies and their pincers refused to close on our rubber-gloved fingers. Trying to detect movement, we scrutinized their mantis-like faces and watched the tiny jaws saw feebly back and forth. What a waste, I thought. These creatures had been pulled upward from two, three, or four hundred feet of water into freezing air, starved and hauled en masse, only to be dumped back into the ocean.

We switched valves on the pump and began to empty the saltwater from the hold. I unbolted the hatch covers. Wanting it to appear like any other delivery, I stood on deck and took slow pulls of coffee from my mug. Two cannery workers in yellow and orange rain gear climbed down the dock ladder and hopped aboard our boat. With a shrill thumb-and-forefinger whistle they signaled the crane operator to lower the first empty tote. Jumping into the hold onto the backs of the crab, they kicked at the sapless mass beneath them, to make room for their feet, then bent down and stared at the tarnished bodies.

I held a swig of coffee between my tongue and the back of my teeth. The workers looked briefly at each other and one of them caught my eye. I swung my mug in a half salute and lifted my eyebrows with what I hoped was a noncommittal gesture. As they waited for a signal to unload, one of them picked up a crab and jabbed its face with his gloved finger. I turned away and swallowed the mouthful of tepid coffee. Finally, I heard the dull, chitinous ring of shell against aluminum.

Hal asked me to go up to the scales and record the weight of each tote. I scrambled up the ladder and walked inside the high-ceilinged warehouse. It isn't just the size of these big buildings that makes one feel so small, it's how every sound is sucked away from its source, bounced briefly among the rafters and swallowed. The ghosts of my footfalls echoed across the concrete floor.

The forklift arrived. Each container was weighed, then

lifted off the scale and placed in one of two long rows. Our catch stood next to the one from the *Ruff & Ready*. It was a pathetic contrast—the quick and the dying. Then a tall, clean-shaven man in rubber boots but without the ubiquitous rain gear walked by, a clipboard tucked under his arm. As he passed our queue of totes he halted.

Though I'd caught plenty of crab, my last vision of them before heading back to the fishing grounds was of vibrant crustaceans, not the limp mass of bodies in front of me. Questions that had eluded me came flooding in.

To what degree do we traumatize the females and undersize males that are flung like discuses back over the rail? Hauled from stable temperatures at the ocean's bottom up to the chilling air in minutes, then landing with a hard smack on the water's surface, could even the toughest not be adversely affected? What of those that are left too long on deck, and lose legs to the cold? What disadvantage would they have in securing food, in escaping predators? Could weakened immune systems cause an inability to fight disease, like the one attacking the eggs of the female kings?

What authority the man with the clipboard possessed I never learned. He turned and walked through an open doorway with a determined stride. As we pulled away from the cannery I asked, "Does this mean they took them?" Hal, sounding equally amazed, shrugged. "I guess." It was not until almost two months later, when he handed me a check, that my question was answered.

The 1989 season was a cold one. A Siberian high swung down over much of Alaska and remained for weeks, producing wind chills as low as minus forty on the waters near Kodiak.

Later I learned that it was the strongest high-pressure system ever recorded in North America. Our pump froze and had to be brought inside the cabin to thaw. Ice formed on the wooden false deck and encased the hydraulic puller in a shroud of rimy white. It plugged scuppers and turned the lines into slippery yellow serpents. The cod we used as bait were hard as bricks. To force the steel hooks through them, I had to pilot a hole with an old hand drill, spinning the wooden handle round and round like an eggbeater while I pinned the fish against the deck with my knees. The cold penetrated our boots and gloves, forcing us to swing our arms and jog in place, making a midday switch into dry gloves and liners imperative.

On the evening of January 23 a report came over the SSB radio that someone had been injured in the Bering Sea aboard the processor *Pacific Challenger.* There is an instant and utter seriousness that sweeps the fleet when a Mayday call is heard. Hands reach out to turn the volume up and normal transmissions stop. The man was crushed up to his pelvis between two conveyor belts. Listening to his vital signs being relayed to the Coast Guard operators in Kodiak, we knew it was grim: pulse feathery and erratic, blood pressure low and dropping fast. I leaned over the galley counter, stunned by the Coast Guard operator's litany of questions. He wanted to know the name and address of the vessel owner, the port of registry, and the vessel's color.

My God, I thought, a man is dying here—DO SOMETHING! Get a doctor on the line, suggest some form of first aid. Ask about the damn color later!

We waited anxiously for each subsequent report of vital signs. There was a foreboding hum in the long pauses between transmissions. Minutes slipped by, and with them the man's chances. I tried to imagine my body forced into some hideous shape by the maw of a steel and rubber machine.

The man's blood pressure plummeted and his pulse disappeared. After what seemed like hours, someone aboard the *Pacific Challenger* declared him dead. Then the Coast Guard operator, in the same unhurried tone, asked the credentials of the person who had made the pronouncement. I was not kneeling next to the victim with my fingers pressed to his carotid artery, but I felt anger well up inside me. Everyone listening knew the certainty of the situation.

I looked out the window and caught a glimpse of my own mortality mirrored off the undulating waves. My thoughts held briefly in the surface tension of the water, then dissipated upward, downward, and out.

After the Coast Guard operator signed off, the channel was cleared for normal use. Then a strange thing happened. Nothing. It wasn't silence exactly, but the low harmonic buzz left by the absence of transmissions. The hush continued, a tribute to the man lost, to the vagaries of nautical life and perhaps to our own good fortune. How right it would be for the lull to last all night, to check the impulse to press on, to fish, to make a profit. Minutes passed. Then with a sound like the crack of a whip, someone keyed his microphone. *Marietta* wye77 *Marietta . . . this is* wke85 *Kodiak . . . go to Channel 4417.* Soon other sets of letters and numbers hailed other letters and numbers, and they too switched frequencies. Though we did not follow to listen in, we knew the drift of the conversations. There would be talk of latitude and longitude and millibars. There would be estimates of wave height and wind direction. Captains would disguise the size of their catch with a secret code issued by their canneries. It was just one of many codes of the sea.

The years took a toll on my body. One season Hal acquired lines that refused to coil properly and we fought them fathom after fathom. Tendonitis turned my left hand into a stiff claw that I used like a hook to guide the line around and around in increasingly sloppy circles. My right hand was weak and painful. I feared I would soon lose what little remained of its strength.

But it was my back that literally brought me to my knees. I tried anything to keep from bending at the waist. It must have looked as if a plank were strapped to my spine, the way I dropped to my right knee for a coil of line or to secure the grappling hook. Pain knifed my lower back every time I picked crab or hung new bait jars. When it was my turn to crawl down into the dark and confined lazarette to grab another fifty-pound box of frozen herring, I was glad Hal and Scott couldn't see my face twist with agony as I wrestled the waxed box toward daylight.

At night in my narrow bunk, with numbness singing down my left leg, I embraced the hours before dawn. Each day brought new misery, but I stubbornly resolved to see the season through. Then, with barely a week to go, I conceded. One morning I extracted myself from my sleeping bag with considerable effort and rolled to the floor between the bunks. From a pile at my side, I grabbed my pants and threw them to my feet, then clumsily hooked my right big toe through the belt loop and tried to guide my jeans over my left foot. Hal saw me fumbling and asked, "Do you want some help?"

"If I can't get my damn pants on, just throw me in the crab pot for bait!" My feeble attempt at humor couldn't hide my disgust and embarrassment. By now, it was clear that I was a liability for Hal and Scott. Hal assured me they could finish the season and put the gear away without me. That afternoon, the *Windigo* was returning to port and I could catch a ride with Robbie and crew.

I picture myself on the ride back to Kodiak, a young man of medium height with a full reddish beard, wearing his bright blue *Stormy Seas* jacket. He leans slightly against the teak counter, the one position that eases the excruciating stabs of pain in his lower back. He looks out at the water of Viekoda Bay. Its color this time of year resembles unpolished turquoise.

What is he thinking? Probably not of all the other men, women, youths, middle-aged or elderly, Caucasian, Asian, Russian, Aleut, or a mix, who risk injury and even their lives for adventure or wages. Not of the crab scuttling along the ocean floor, methodically scavenging for clams, worms, fish parts, snails, and shrimp. Nor of the impact that the year's 4.7 million pound quota would have on their population, of the way the fisheries target one species until it is nearly depleted, then move on to the next, and the next.

No, his thoughts are more mundane. He is only a common man trying to survive, preoccupied with his own pain.

He is thinking of the hour-long flight to Anchorage, followed by another hour and a half on the road before he can stretch out in his own bed. He wants to believe that within a week, he'll be splitting and hauling firewood, sheet rocking the downstairs bedroom or skijoring the back trails with

his dog Jäger. Yet the intensity of the pain makes him wonder if he will be limited to a sales job at the local hardware
store. He is hoping that Hal and Scott understand the last
thing he wanted was to leave early. He is thinking about loy-
alty and friendship and the need for money, and how difficult it can be to do a job you love.

6

Field Test

My friend Are (pronounced R-E and rhymes with starry) and I were on board a commercial fishing boat returning from the Bering Sea off the coast of southwest Alaska. After three weeks of stacking corks, scraping herring scales off our rain gear, and jockeying for position with other boats, we were feeling a little giddy and more than ready to return to civilization.

On the long boat ride from Togiak back to Port Lions we had plenty of time to discuss some of our favorite topics: airplanes, knots, and outdoor gear. We started with airplanes. Are, being the proud owner of a Citabria, pointed out its numerous excellent features and the fact that the name is airbatic (a form of aerobatic) spelled backwards. I suppose my response will not go down in the annals of Cub driver's rebuttals when I countered that Piper Super Cub backwards is Repip Bucrepus.

Deep into a discussion and display of knots, the two of us stood on the flying bridge of the *Marci La Rae* on the ride across Shelikof Strait.

"I see your clove hitch with a sheepshank and raise you a carrick bend," I said. Are was soon over my head with his knot-ical knowledge, so I latched onto our mutual yet dormant interest in climbing and turned the conversation to the prussik. Multiple prussik knots are sometimes used for ascending and descending a rope.

Talk turned to action. In a moment of inspiration Are

secured himself to the rigging and started up. Unfortunately, something jammed on the way down. He hung there like
a polar fleece windsock in a five-knot breeze; behind him,
Kodiak Island was a distant smudge on the horizon.

Of course, I came to his aid—that is, when I finally pulled
myself off the deck where I had collapsed in a fit of laughter. And not before I ran down to my bunk to retrieve my
camera.

Are's bivouac bag (a tent-like shell designed to protect a sleeping bag from the elements) was the source of much pride:
made in California, it was the Mercedes Benz of bivvies.
It never leaked, it was built for a lifetime. So when I mentioned I'd just purchased a bivvy bag from a rival company,
he snickered. "I hear they're *fairly* good."

After the season, Are stayed with me for a few days at my
house in the Mat-Su Valley before returning south. The cool
spring day turned into a drizzly night. "Maybe we should field-
test the bags." I pointed to the rain-splattered deck beyond
the sliding glass door. Instead of comfortable beds for the
first time in five weeks, we settled on wet two-by-sixes.

I wriggled in and waited for sleep to come. Although my
bag didn't leak, raindrops hit the deck and splashed up into
my face. My options were to close the bag completely to stay
bone-dry and possibly suffocate, or leave an opening big
enough to breathe. I chose the latter, though it meant catching a lot of spray. I drifted in and out of sleep and after a few
hours became aware of two things: Are hadn't moved, and
I needed to visit the bathroom.

Stealthily I unzipped my bag. I didn't want Are to catch
me going inside and think, even for an instant (not that it

was a contest, mind you) that he had won. Quietly as I could I stood up, bare feet on wet wood. I watched over my shoulder, but there was no movement from Are as the door slid in its track. He was sleeping so soundly inside that nylon cocoon I was envious. I made my first step into the semi-dark living room. All quiet. Second step. Nothing. On the third step the floor squeaked. I shot a glance to the lumpy outline on the patio. Not even a twitch.

Then from the couch came a sleepy voice. "I suppose you think I'm a wimp." Startled, I reached over and flipped on a light switch. "What are you doing?" I asked.

"My bag needs a new application of seam-sealer," he admitted.

"Well, Are, even a Mercedes needs occasional maintenance," I said, and feeling a bit generous added, "It isn't nasty enough outside for a real test anyway." I pulled open the door and dragged our bivvies inside. There was no need to humiliate my friend. Besides, I still had the photos of him stuck in the rigging.

7

Exxon Summer

By the time I arrived in Port Lions on the northwest side of Kodiak Island in April of 1989, almost a month had passed since the *Exxon Valdez* began spewing crude oil into the pristine waters of Prince William Sound. Although I'd heard reports of ankle-deep oil, sea otters desperately grooming their matted fur in an attempt to keep warm, and eagles dehydrated by ingested oil, the massive cleanup effort was 300 miles away and far from my thoughts. I was bound for the Bering Sea, to fish herring near Togiak. Or so I thought.

Within days of my arrival an Exxon representative approached Hal with an offer to hire his boat, the *Marci La Rae*.

Hal didn't want to make the decision alone. His words—"Whatever you guys want to do"—echoed in the boat's cabin as I sat across the table from fellow crewmembers Are and Tom. Looking out at Settler Cove, with its towering spruce and rugged cliffs rising just above the boat harbor, it was hard to imagine that oil from the sound could disrupt this peaceful setting.

We debated. Hanging out in Port Lions for a week or two to make some quick cash, then having a try at the herring was unrealistic. In order to be on the fishing grounds before the season started, we needed to prepare the boat and gear and leave right away. Though Hal had once made the trip from Port Lions to Togiak in eighty-six hours straight, his longest trip lasted fourteen weather-plagued days. To make money in Bristol Bay, we would first need to cover expenses of insurance, fuel, and food. With short openings and lots of competition, making big money on herring was a roll of the dice. Though I wanted to experience the Togiak fishery, I agreed with Tom and Are, who were both experienced fishermen, to sign on with Exxon. As crewmembers, we would each make around $200 a day. Hal, as boat owner and captain, would get nearly seven times that much. The drawback was that there was no time commitment. We could work for two days or 200.

The job was a reunion cruise of sorts for Tom, Hal, and me. I couldn't think of anyone I'd rather work with. We'd all grown up on the hillside above Anchorage, attended the same grade school and junior high, and graduated from high school together.

Tom was now a happy family man and a successful contractor in Kodiak. As kids, we shared time on bikes and skis and in canoes. Swarms of mosquitoes and soggy sleeping bags never got him down. Tom was the same indefatigable optimist who once had three of us bouncing up and down in the bow of his overloaded skiff for ten miles trying to get it on step. He was the same minimizer of hardships who, after a grueling bivouac one late fall night on storm-battered Malina Point, concluded that he was fortunate because he "had a plastic bag to crawl into."

Hal was the stable one. He moved with confidence on deck in the harshest conditions. His calm demeanor masked a past of aggressive alpine skiing and fearless driving, his hands locked on the steering wheel of his Triumph GT6 as it rumbled along Alaskan highways. A natural curiosity led him to absorb things easily, and he shared his knowledge willingly.

Other fishermen often sought his advice on a finicky water pump or a troublesome battery switch. The only flaw in his personality actually made life easier for those around him. He worried too much. When the autopilot failed or when we needed to re-route the plumbing, Hal would rise in the morning with bleary eyes after sleepless hours of horizontal engineering, an imaginary blueprint above his bunk. The rest of us slept soundly until the smell of perking coffee permeated the cabin.

Are was a sailor with a Norseman's affinity for the sea. He could fuss in the galley for hours with a cheesecake or grind happily away on fiberglass, throwing up plumes of dust. He read literature and quoted long passages from Monty Python movies with equal alacrity. I connected immediately with his appreciation for the incongruities of life.

There was genuine concern at the safety meeting held in the Port Lions community building. For most of the people seated around me, their livelihoods and their futures were at stake. Still, there was a sense that the meeting was a formality, as if few believed oil would actually hit.

A load of supplies arrived at the ferry dock. Soon the deck of the *Marci La Rae* was loaded and we spent part of one day moving 3,500 feet of bright yellow boom around Peregrebni Point to the new boat harbor in Settler Cove. As we inventoried and organized the anchors, lines, and strobes provided by Exxon, I had the sense that we were part of a well-prepared operation.

We were put on "oil watch." For eighteen days we were scouts, looking for signs of oil in the waters near Port Lions. No one on our crew seemed particularly excited until the fifth day, when we found four oil-slicked murres in Duck Bay on Afognak Island. The birds' white bellies were no longer white; their feathers clung together in a black mass. Held in the hand, the murres seemed smaller than I'd imagined, and so removed from living creatures it was as if they had never taken flight or dived or breathed.

Seaweed is what had kept them afloat, perhaps all the way from Prince William Sound. Oil robs feathers of their buoyancy and most affected pelagic birds sink to the bottom. We slipped their cold bodies into plastic bags and turned our gaze toward the horizon to search for more. But whatever dread or excitement we felt soon waned.

Each morning Hal phoned Exxon headquarters in Kodiak, then relayed the day's directive to us on the boat. Assignments trickled in: replace batteries on strobes marking a log boom that protected Barabara Cove, cruise the waters around Whale Island, survey Danger Bay, exchange one type of boom for another.

In order to cover a greater area and get a better perspective, Hal offered the use of his Cessna 180. Tom, Are, and I, along with Hal's brother-in-law Robbie, took turns flying as observer in the passenger's seat. We flew as far as Afognak and Shuyak Islands looking for sheen. Those of us left in Port Lions looked for activities to alleviate our boredom.

We scraped and sanded old varnish off the boat's teak rails. We built a crow's nest and Are concentrated on fiberglassing it. Tom and I persuaded Hal to allow us to finish the exterior of his house with beveled cedar siding. Every other morning we went jogging past the dump and the old cemetery out to the airstrip and back. In wet, foggy evenings we played basketball on the school's cracked cement

court, barely outscoring the young boys we towered over.
We played guitar and sang, checked out the tiny library,
and attended a local talent show. Part of me felt we should
take *standby* more literally—standing on the gunnels of the
boat ready to cast off. But we were never more than fifteen
minutes away, and could easily drop what we were doing
if necessary.

While docked at Port Lions, Hal stayed at his house with
his wife and son. On board, Are and Tom were ideal ship-
mates. We worked around the cramped quarters, kept our
gear on our own bunks, and used individual Walkmans to
listen to music. I was the designated cook, while Are and
Tom took turns at dishes. Are told stories of trekking in the
Southwest. Tom and I relived old times and caught up on
the years we hadn't seen each other. We were like family.
We didn't feel lucky to be in each other's company, we just
found it easy to be ourselves.

With Hal back on the *Marci La Rae* we continued our search
for oil by boat. On Wednesday, May 10, we found clumps of
oil in Raspberry Strait, bobbing like brown cow patties amid
a line of kelp. Unfortunately we hadn't been instructed on
how to recover oil once we found it. Although World War II
Navy skimmers (boats that had pumps to handle the thick
oil) were said to be en route, rumors were that they were
not hours, but days, away.

We unofficially promoted ourselves from "oil watch" to
"oil recovery." With an impromptu designer's ingenuity,
Hal grabbed a five-gallon deck bucket and cut the bottom
out, then attached a section of herring seine to the inverted rim. A length of driftwood served as a handle. With the

improvised net we ladled almost forty gallons of oil into a 55-gallon drum double-lined with sky-blue, industrial-strength plastic bags.

There was an air of satisfaction on the return trip to Port Lions. However crude the tool, we had found a simple way to do some good. Back in town, we went immediately to the dump, scrounging materials for more "Vada Goober Scoopers," as someone dubbed them. I recall the term was pig-Norwegian for "water snot scoopers" or something equally visceral. But years later, Are, our Scandinavian linguist, claimed no credit.

For the remainder of May the hull of the *Marci La Rae* wore a dark brown smudge at her waterline. More local boats and crews were hired. Air traffic increased as pilots directed boats below them. Although we used boom to block sheen and tarballs from sensitive areas or to collect oil when the wind and seas were down, much of our work was slip in, scoop, and go. From the flying bridge someone would point and shout, "Looks like a line of mousse nuggets over there!" We referred to the clusters of small tarballs as mousse—the common term for a frothy water-in-oil emulsion—because moose nuggets were something familiar to us all, and a bit of humor helped us through the dirty work. Hal would idle alongside as we'd recover remnants of the 11 million gallons spilled, sometimes only ounces at a time.

On the morning of May 18 near Gori Point, on the south side of Raspberry Island, we located a dark serpentine line of tarballs mixed in with kelp. We had been in Kupreanof Strait for the past two days scooping up dozens of dead birds and scattered oil. Though we had found a layering of oil on the western beaches of Deranof Island and scooped and bagged from early morning until 10 p.m., we hadn't yet seen anything like this thick-bodied python tracing the shoreline.

A west wind pushed the oil closer to land by the minute. The swells were big enough to render a boom useless—and there wasn't enough room to deploy it if we'd been able to. Hal worked the controls from the flying bridge, until the *Marci La Rae* was parallel to the swells. We braced our legs against the boat's constant swing. Sweat soon beaded our faces as we labored at a frenetic pace to gather the oil. I bent over the rail, watching the dark blobs rise and fall, gathering up one or two at a time, fighting the first feelings of nausea.

Until today, the tarballs congealed by the cool ocean water had left little residue on the web of our Vada Goober Scoopers as we pulled them aboard. But now, the sun broiled down, revealing the adhesive nature of the oil. We poured gasoline—the only solvent we had to clean the crude off our tools—into the bottom of an open 55-gallon drum. When a scooper turned too gummy, we staggered across the deck to the drum, plunged it to the bottom and swished it around while fumes rushed past our faces, inundating our eyes and nostrils. Fuzzy-templed, I leaned against the drum's rim, steadying myself against the vapors and the increasing roll of the boat. Tom's face drained of color and the sparkle left his eyes. Are pressed on, mum. For me it became a blur, like the spin-dry effect of a night in college, saturated with tequila and beer. Our cast-iron-stomached captain was too valuable at the controls to help us much.

As I glanced out in my stupefied state, I could see the shape of the *Windigo* dancing in the heat waves off our stern. Other boats were in the area and there was a steady drone from spotter airplanes above. By late afternoon we had to abandon our effort. The seas were building. We transferred the nearly eight hundred pounds of crude we'd collected that day along with several bags of dead, oiled birds onto the *Ocean Hope 1*. We guessed the birds were not local casualties, but tarred and feathered victims that had drifted down from the sound. My head still throbbed as we anchored near Wisher's beach on Kodiak Island.

The bow of the *Marci La Rae* pointed at the sloped, rocky beach. We noticed it was lacquered with a thin coat of oil. Through our radio check that evening, we learned we had set an unofficial record for the amount of oil recovered that day: highliners in an obscene fishery.

Whop, whop, whop echoed through the salt air. A helicopter swept into view, hovered, and then landed on the beach. An Exxon representative crawled out. Bent forward at the waist, he hurried away from the rotors' blast, slipped on the slickened rocks, and fell on his butt. He got up, took a few strides toward Hal, and shook his hand. They spoke briefly in the din of the idling chopper, then they turned, climbed aboard, and were airborne.

Hal returned from his ride with news that oil had hit the rocks near the place we'd labored all day. With stronger winds in the forecast, more oil was soon to follow. *Sacrificial beach* was the term we learned that evening: the surrender of one beach for the sake of another. Sometimes a mandate was given for a crew to direct oil to a specific area. But today the weather determined which shores were hit and which were spared. I crawled into my bunk still queasy from the morning's noxious vapors.

Wind and waves broke up the concentration of oil in Kupreanof. We moved on to Raspberry Cape, Malina Point and Paramanof, Anton Larsen, and Selief Bays. Over the next week, in addition to birds and tarballs, we found small, white particles, often accompanied by a luminescent, rainbow-colored sheen. They looked like bath oil beads. Held between thumb and forefinger they squished to a waxy smear. Oil dispersant, someone speculated. By now it was two months old and many miles from where it was dumped. It dotted the waters near Whale Pass where a pod of humpbacks energetically fed on krill.

When June arrived, Tom and I, who had only signed on for the herring season, were to be replaced by Hal's salmon crew. Tom and his family owned a beach site near Port Bailey and they needed to gear up their set-net site for salmon fishing. Are would continue on.

Another change was on the horizon. Exxon had asked Hal to turn the *Marci La Rae* into a test-fish vessel. The boat would be cleaned spotless, equipped to seine, and then fish at predetermined sites. A biologist would be assigned to live on board, record the number and type of fish, and take scale samples from the catch.

It seemed a good time to leave. Tom was going and the reunion was over. But a wave of melancholy swept over me. It felt like those Sunday afternoons in early fall, when, as a youth, I wandered the swamps near home. I did not want to leave the comfort of the woods to return to school, as now I was reluctant to leave the boat, my friends, a job unfinished.

I figured how much I would make if I could stay on until fall: five figures. I both wanted and needed the money. I had just taken out two loans to buy a used airplane. And I was jealous. It didn't seem fair that Are and hundreds of others would continue to scoop up the dollars. Why not me? I felt greedy, and guilty for feeling so. But there was another reason: I wasn't ready to abandon ship.

This reunion of friends had brought back the sense of innocence of my earlier years. There was a directness of communication between us, a sense of belonging that made me wonder if I had missed something as an only child. Was this what it felt like to have brothers? I liked the men Tom and Hal had become.

May 30. We began cleanup of the containment boom, boat, and gear, wiping off the oil with solvent and rags. Hal took the skiff to Anton Larsen Bay, then drove to Kodiak to attend a meeting. He returned that afternoon disheartened. He would be working under the Alaska Department of Fish and Game and they wanted to renegotiate the contract, lower the pay dramatically. What had seemed like a promotion for doing a good job suddenly felt like a demotion.

Ambivalence swept over me the next morning as I assisted in hooking up the seine block. Though I knew we were paid more than the job called for, I hated the sense of being devalued. But it didn't matter. My time was about to end. I said good-bye to Tom when Hal took him back to Kodiak.

Hal returned with two bits of news. The boat owners had formed a coalition and would stand up to department representatives the next day. Also, my replacement would stay for several weeks on another boat. I could continue working on the *Marci La Rae*.

Mark, a Port Lions resident in his early twenties, filled Tom's place. Rail-thin with long, dark, curly hair, Mark looked like a rock star and played in a local band. He brought an electric guitar on board and listened to music I'd never heard before. He was also an experienced fisherman.

We were introduced to Ed, the biologist-technician assigned to our boat. Tall and athletic, Ed was pleasant and well spoken. He had a degree in biology but admitted that so many technicians were being hired any degree would suffice. Space was tight on board and there was no place for Ed to sleep. We laid plywood down over the galley table, transforming it into a bed each night, stowing it away each morning.

After some tense negotiations, Hal and the other boat owners signed new contracts that were almost as lucrative as the old ones. We would be covering an area of the Alaska Peninsula; Puale Bay was our first destination.

On the eleven-hour run across Shelikof Strait, patches of sheen periodically calmed the water's surface. We were instructed to fish only if there were no signs of oil nearby. It seemed reasonable. If we used a soiled net we chanced contaminating the fish, rendering our samples worthless.

Near Terrace Island we caught the first sockeye. Ed did a quick visual inspection and removed a few scales. The fish appeared fresh and robust. We worked our way up and down the coast, fishing where we could. I scribbled notes in my journal as we moved from one site to the next:

JUNE 6
Sheen and some tarballs near the Puale rocks.

JUNE 9
Kilokak-sheen, white particles & small tarballs scattered throughout the area.

JUNE 11
Kanatak Lagoon to Kilokak—a lot of light sheen & some mousse—didn't make any sets.

We traded eggs, tomatoes, and an old newspaper for strawberry ice cream with the crew of another boat. Muffins and brownies made us fat. We feasted on halibut, black bass, and Dolly Varden. As the need arose, we changed engine oil and gear lube, fixed the water pump and the autopilot. We bathed in small lakes, walked flotsam-littered beaches, and snapped photos of seagull eggs and shipwrecks. We sang songs, wrote letters, and began enjoying Mark's music selections.

We worked our way farther south. It was all new and exciting country to me: Agripina Bay, Port Wrangell, Yantarni Bay, Aniakchak Bay, Kujulik Bay. Are and I created our own myth: twin sisters who inhabited Kumlik Island. It would be a double date and I would, of course, get the taller one. As we motored by at ten knots we would shout to the imaginary girls that we would return soon. At each passing, as the small island faded in our wake, we swore, next time, we would stop and visit the Kumlik twins.

Near Unavikshak Island we found the largest tarball of the summer, the size of a volleyball. Unavikshak was just over thirty miles from the protected waters of Chignik Lagoon, home to one of the most lucrative sockeye fisheries on earth. We motored in through the narrow channel and tied up near the Aleutian Dragon cannery. Everyone we met wanted to know what was going on. The word was out that we were the forerunners of the "oil" fleet.

People were hungry for answers. Mixed with their curiosity were looks of steely hostility that pierced us like a gaff hooks. At first I couldn't understand this reaction. Then it dawned on me: our reports could cause the state officials to cancel the salmon opener scheduled in two days. I translated the stares we received from under the bills of worn baseball caps: *Tell us it's okay—or just go away.*

The next day, the biologist in charge of the local fishery rode around the lagoon with us. Finding it clean, he gave approval to a captain of a local boat to make a test set. The catch yielded over 2,000 fish and the excitement was palpable. The next morning a bright orange flare trailing blue-gray smoke arched over the water, marking the exact moment fishing could begin. A helicopter sliced the air just above radio antennas that rose high over crows' nests. Diesel engines belched thick clouds of exhaust as boats jockeyed for position and power skiffs dragged nets off decks, forming them into imperfect circles.

There in the northeast shadow of Veniaminof Volcano, the Aleutian Range held snow in high bowls, in the lee of ridges, and gullies that cut almost down to the water's edge. Gray hues of clouds and patchy fog dulled peaks, streambed, beach, and brush. Just outside of the lagoon we found some sheen as we headed north to Hook Bay. We were 460 miles from the site of the spill, and still we had not outdistanced the oil.

On a warm sunny day we dropped anchor in a small bight on the west side of Sutwick Island. Someone spotted an adolescent brown bear ambling south on the beach. The bear was golden brown with chocolate-hued leggings.

With the gait of a limber athlete, it strolled and poked its nose under rocks and driftwood, its long, sleek hair undulating like thick beach grass in an afternoon breeze. The bruin stopped as the shore pulled him close to our boat. I thought he might turn and retrace his steps. Then he eased himself into the water. It looked as if he was tired of walking the beach and I thought he might swim across to the other side of the tiny half-moon bay. Instead he rolled onto his back and floated, bobbing slowly in the gentle surf. The sun glinted off of his wet fur as he poked and slapped kelp, oblivious to us, to anything outside his small circle of now; a bear with the soul of an otter and the innocence of a child.

My fondest memory of the Exxon summer is the Sutwick bear. I recall wanting to slip into the salt water beside him, float on my back and point my toes to the sky. Watching him, it was easy to forget about tarballs and sheen. It was easy to imagine floating forever.

I wonder now why my predominant feeling from those months working on the Exxon spill cleanup is one of joy? How could bagging up hundreds of dead birds and countless gallons of oil not overshadow the whole experience?

It's a matter of distance, I suppose. We were hundreds of miles from the disaster's front line; the birds we found were dead, not struggling to live; eagles were soaring, not sick. There were no snails, barnacles, and chitons falling off the rocks, no baby sea otters succumbing to the effects of ingested crude. I was with buddies, and we were working on an important job—together.

I would like to be able to say, over two decades later, that every negative effect from the spill has passed, that ecological disasters are history, and that a collective intellect has replaced human greed.

What I can say is that Are, Tom, Hal, and I are still friends. It is a profound gift, the real fortune I made that brief summer.

Two

Guiding Days

Searching within the Archipelago

8

It was never about the killing. I was drawn to any occupa-tion that would allow me to place my boot in the track of a brown bear, listen to the bellowing of rutting moose, or curl up at four thousand feet in a shallow depression still pun-gent with the aroma of sheep. At one time, I had even con-sidered becoming a field geologist, but my paleontology pro-fessor hinted I might be better at identifying live animals than ones long dead. More by luck than design, through a series of fortuitous yet minor events, I was pulled along an ever-deepening trail toward the title of big game guide.

Though my initiation had come in the mountains and muskeg of the western slopes of the Alaska Range, in the spring of 1979 I was searching for brown bear in southeast-ern Alaska. On the commercial flight into Juneau, I listened intently to my mentor and boss, Stan Frost, describe the country I was about to see for the first time in my guiding career. To a terrestrial nimrod such as myself, boat hunt-ing within the Alexander Archipelago seemed as exotic as the names implied: Baranof, Chichagof, Kuiu.

Our skipper, Tom Parks, who had navigated these waters for decades, exuded the confidence of a man at home in his element. Charts tucked into a newly oiled teak rack, bunks crisply folded, lines neatly coiled on deck, windows spotless, everything displayed a master's touch. Even the coffee was percolated and poured with care.

On the eve of our first client's arrival, we sat on the hatch covers luxuriating in the rhythmic dip and sway of the ocean, while the *Tiller Tramp* worked against its mooring lines. Glaucous-winged gulls peered from the rigging at the wisps of smoke spiraling up from Stan's corncob pipe. The familiar rum and maple aroma added a strange sweetness to the algae-rich air of the harbor. Tom's eyes glinted, mirroring the phosphorescent backdrop of small life forms swimming erratically in the dark water. As Tom and Stan relived their past hunts together, I felt in the presence of two sages: one of the sea, the other of the mountains. With such an auspicious beginning to our saltwater safari, it seemed as if nothing could dampen the prospect of a successful season.

The following day the weather took a sour turn. Heavy rain sliced the afternoon as Stan introduced me to our hunter, who brusquely shook my hand and presented me the back of his brand new PVC-over-polyester slicker. I swallowed hard, quietly picked up his duffel bags and deposited them next to his bunk.

"Buffleheads, aren't they?" The hunter gestured across the bow of our skiff. My binoculars were trained on a curious brown object partially obscured in the tall grass just above the high-water mark. A stump. Glancing over at the squat birds, the drakes with the distinctive white blaze dominating their bulky heads, I was impressed. He seemed to know ducks. Already he had identified goldeneye, scoters, oldsquaw, and pintail. We slowly motored around the next point, my attention divided between searching the water for reefs and scanning the beach for bear.

Maybe I had misjudged his distracted stare as we chipped aqua-blue chunks from floating icebergs for our coolers, as we explored isolated bays and felt the spray of a thundering waterfall mix with the dense salt air. Perhaps it was only a matter of semantics, how he always substituted the word *kill* for the word *hunt*: "Sure would like to kill a sheep some-day." But his word choice bothered me. *Kill* was not the term that I immediately associated with hunting. Seek, pursue, search, yes. That the holistic aspects of hunting, the blood and beauty, the death and wonder should be reduced to such a harsh-sounding verb seemed an affront to the ani-mals and country.

As the next stretch of beach came into view I hit the off switch on the idling Evinrude.

"Damn it, I wish I'd brought my shotgun. Those are har-lequins!" His face pressed into his binoculars. "Shouldn't have listened to Stan!" His fist slammed the side of the skiff. The hollow tremor echoing from the aluminum seemed to launch him into a tirade. It had something to do with not securing a special permit from a museum back east. "With that I can kill anything I want, anytime I want!"

There seemed little percentage in entering into a dia-logue with him about the ethics of hunting. In later years, I would have done so. But then, realizing my handling of the situation could affect our relationship over the next week, I offered, "Well, you know there is a fall hunt for ducks and I'm sure you'd be able to make arrangements with one of the local guides." My words drifted aimlessly over the ocean swells, waved away like annoying insects.

I didn't know what else to say. At an inch over six feet, he stood a good three inches above me, his close-cropped thatch of pale brown hair in contrast to the ample spread of his belly. I wondered how he perceived me. With my scuffed hip boots, bent pack frame, and rifle's thin bluing, it was apparent that I'd had a few years in the field, though even a full auburn beard couldn't hide the youthfulness of my twenty-four-year-old face.

The tiller of the outboard rested against my knee as if urging me to move on. I turned the handle to the start position, squeezed the bulb on the hose, and gave the cord a hard pull. I eyed the gas tank, determining that we could cruise along another forty-five minutes before making our way back to Tom's boat.

The following day we motored around Walker Point and headed into Murder Cove on the southern end of Admiralty Island. On one of these beaches in 1869, a party of fur traders had been robbed and killed by local natives. The stories Tom told last night were fascinating, but the duck man spent the time doodling blue ink stars on the napkin resting on the galley table. Now, as he stared blankly at some point just above the horizon, I glassed the first beach, thinking it could have been a morning just like this that the fur traders spent their last hours sleeping, their bodies pressed wearily into the sand.

A bald eagle glided past our skiff and landed deftly near the tip of a Sitka spruce. The hunter raised his rifle and peered through the scope. It was odd, given that yesterday he seemed comfortable enough with binoculars, which, in this terrain, were the superior optics. Then I saw his finger on the trigger.

Stan's edict, enforced by his guides, was to always have an empty chamber until the final stages of a stalk. This policy was made clear in correspondence, pre-hunt talks, and constant reminders. It could not be misinterpreted, but it could be disregarded. If there was ever a time to state the obvious it was now. "You know, of course, that you can't shoot those."

I half expected a comeback, an argument that eagles were mere scavengers, but the hunter only grunted and lowered his gun. I glassed the hillsides and beaches wishing I could will a boulder or hummock of grass into *Ursus arctos* and transform the tension I felt into relief. The day continued in strained silence.

As we swung on anchor that night the creak and pop of the line and waves slapping the sturdy hull filled me with dismay. I tried to understand why I hadn't given Stan the full story. With his broad face and high cheekbones, Stan had a classical look of stoicism. How many times had I heard him reply to those guides who expressed discontent with a hunter, "Well, you don't have to marry the guy. You only have to live with him for a week." Yes, but those seven days are made up of over ten thousand minutes. Now each one seemed exponentially longer than the one before it. Yet I was determined not to complain. So I'd dropped a casual remark, the kind of offhand comment we sometimes make when not really expecting a reply, "Boy, I sure hope we see a bear tomorrow, because the hunter seems awfully anxious to shoot something. . . . "

"Crows, can I shoot crows?" The hunter interrupted the stillness. "No, you can't." The third day was proving no better than the previous two. Increasingly tired of his game, I had dropped all explanation or attempt at distraction. It had been the same all morning with porpoise, a kingfisher, and sea otters. No, no, no. I was considering running him back to the *Tiller Tramp* when just beyond the starboard gunwale of the skiff a slate-gray dome emerged from the water, then the entire head of a harbor seal. The fur of its face was stretched tautly over its skull, its eyes haunted and beseeching. The hunter slammed a cartridge into the chamber and raised his rifle to his shoulder.

I flung my weight deliberately to port and began rocking the boat in order to throw off his aim. A series of short-crested waves from the aluminum hull rippled out over the water. The seal was gone. Fighting the impulse to snatch up the seven-foot oar and thwack him on the head, I commanded, "Give me your rifle." Apparently taken aback by my anger, he handed it over. I allowed myself the brief indulgence of imagining what a satisfying splash the rifle would make as it hit the water. Instead, I removed the bolt and dropped it into my coat pocket. Then I returned his rifle. Without a word I jerked the outboard's starter rope, spun the skiff around, and headed for the bight a few miles to the northwest where Stan and Tom were waiting.

A midday return would signal two possibilities to those on board: bad weather or success. A gently rolling swell, light breeze, and high overcast could only mean the latter. In an effort to squelch even the suspicion of celebration, I flashed a thumbs down sign as we eased our way up to the stern.

Tom led the hunter down to the galley while Stan loaded his pipe and bent his lighter's flame into the bowl with a deep pull of breath. I sat down on the aluminum hatch farthest astern, the only access to the dank storage space called the lazarette. Stan had been slow to accept those parts of me—the guitar strummer and writer of verse—that were incongruous with his concept of an Alaskan guide. As I told my story, I wondered if the confidence, the connection I had built with this man through packing heavy loads of moose meat, fleshing hides, and climbing mountains was dissipating into the sea breeze as quickly as the smoke from his pipe. Would he think I was incompetent? Unable to handle testy clients? Stan said simply, "I'll take the hunter out tomorrow." A few beats later he added, "You can help Tom with some chores here on the boat."

"Change your hat, change your luck," my friend Jerry liked to say. If only it were that easy, I would flick my wrist and another hunter would appear. But no amulet, incantation, or headgear would transform him into someone else.

My view of the skiff departing into the first light of day offered no balm for my spirits. As I washed, dried, and put away the breakfast dishes, within me grew a certainty that today, a bear would slip out from the rain forest and offer itself to Stan and *his* hunter. Stan wouldn't see the behavior I'd witnessed. There would be jubilation, an instant camaraderie spawned by a successful hunt. The more I thought about it, the more miserable I felt. "Not much of a guide, that Steve," people would say. Maybe they were right. And maybe what I was seeking was not adventure or wilderness as much as Stan's approval.

But what if I lost this job? There was always my tool belt, the speed square clicking against the twenty-four-ounce framing hammer and studs and rafters to cut, with blue dust rising from a chalkline. The carpentry I did between guiding seasons could be a full-time job. It was honest, satisfying work. Maybe it didn't matter how things turned out on this trip. I was old enough to know that every occupation has its disappointments. The biggest sin would be to allow my experience to be diminished by a man whose field of view was limited to the crosshairs of his rifle's scope.

Late in the afternoon, Stan pulled the skiff alongside and threw me a line. I tied it off to the rail and glanced at the empty floorboards at his feet. No bear. In an odd replay of the previous day, Tom led the hunter below, while Stan and I stood on deck. Stan pulled apart the sections of his pipe and put in a new filter. He stuck the stem in his mouth.

"Strange duck," he began. "As guides, Steve, we don't have to put up with bullshit like this." He paused. "Tomorrow we'll make the run to Juneau and send him home." His shoulders lifted with a breath, then settled slightly. "It's a great life we live, Steve."

He was right. Fresh air, exercise, unsurpassed scenery— we had it all. What other profession would pay me to explore new places, view wildlife, and escape the crowds? I liked the job too because each day's direction was usually dictated by weather. Adjusting my plans to wind, rain, fog, or sun strengthened my bond to the natural world. What I craved, above all, was *immersion* in wilderness, weeks and months at a time spent breathing in the spicy aroma of Labrador tea, tasting the tart explosion of red currants on my tongue, listening to the *kloo-klok* of a raven in flight.

I looked at Stan. He appeared unconcerned with the thousands of dollars he might have to refund, untroubled by an empty bear tag. What had happened between the two of them? I wanted to ask, but remembered how he had earlier requested nothing more from me than I was willing to share. A wave of relief swept over me. Not only would I keep my job, I would not have to compromise my ethics. That day, I learned to put faith in my misgivings, to listen hard to that visceral sense of violation. I learned that unacceptable behavior is just that, and should be immediately and forcefully addressed.

"How about a beer?" Stan asked, lifting the lid on the cooler. He reached in and pulled out two *Prinz Braus,* and with a touch of glass, a silent toast passed between us.

Early the next morning, I asked Stan if I could row the dinghy to shore and walk around for a while. I wandered out of sight of the boat, around a finger of loose rocks, and came upon a long sweep of gravel beach. A minus tide. A rare glimpse of the sun glinted across the exposed round rocks, turning them into a canted cobblestone road. As the sun's rays hit the dampest part of the beach near the water's edge, tiny spouts of water appeared. A few at first, then dozens, then maybe a hundred sparkling geysers. The beach was alive with a pulsing rhythm. I was here for moments like these. As I knelt in the wet sand, the blue-green water inched up and covered the clam holes. A pair of ducks traced the shoreline's contour. They drifted a moment before they stretched and fluttered their wings, then took flight and disappeared beyond the rocky point.

9

The Hard Way Home

Stan and I watched Sacha de Montbel from Paris ungrace-fully squirm into the back seat of the Super Cub. I shook the hand of the gentleman who had been my last hunter of the season. Stan swung into the front seat and glanced at the darkening skies. Looking me in the eye, he spoke the familiar phrase: "I'll be right back to pick you up." Even then I questioned his return. Good intentions wouldn't fly through a snowstorm and neither would Stan. As the airplane disappeared to the west, snow began to fall.

If outfitting has a spirit, it seems that spirit must be a bit of an eccentric, enjoying the contrast of hours or days of waiting with minutes of frantic stuffing and packing. Years before, I noticed that if everything in camp was ready to go, the airplane would be late. Consequently, I had started leaving my sleeping bag unfurled and noticed a marked improvement in the plane arriving as scheduled. Clients often seemed bewildered when I told them to pack up everything except their bedroll and not to touch it until the airplane was actually on the ground. Of course, it didn't always work, but it did seem to help satisfy my clients' craving for some harmless idiosyncratic behavior in their guides—and better stories when they returned home.

Admittedly, I sometimes went out of my way to augment this mystique. Once, about to leave the site of a moose kill and realizing the flat terrain covered with black spruce would make it hard to relocate the meat and antlers, I hung the lower jaw of the moose on the tip of a nearby tree. In response to my client's questioning look, I gave a long, reverent pause and replied, "For the Moose gods." Then I turned, shouldered my pack, and headed for camp. The singular, practical act of hanging that first jaw easily turned to ritual. In time more ceremony was added and my explanation was shortened to "Moose gods," delivered in a near whisper and only when asked. I briefly pondered the threshold that ritual must transcend to become religion.

The weather grounded such lofty thoughts. Snow was now falling in huge flakes, severely limiting visibility and ruining my chances of returning to the lodge for dinner. In the nearly depleted food box there was only half a bag of pancake mix, a few ounces of cooking oil, some Tang, and tea. I filled the Coleman stove with the last of the white gas and fried up a stack of pancakes. Tang turned out to be a surprisingly tasty alternative to syrup, especially when everything was washed down with a couple of mugs of tea. After slipping into my sleeping bag, I easily fell asleep.

I woke in a tent narrowed by snow, which was still falling heavily. Glancing at the radio in the corner of the tent, I realized there would be no sense calling the lodge even if the battery was charged. But it had been dead for more than a week and there was nothing to do but wait. Outside, the snow was up to my knees and showed no signs of stopping. I quickly cleared the load from the canvas and nestled back in my sleeping bag where I began rereading the novel I had finished the week before. The book had been little more than a sleeping pill on the first read; it was impossible to swallow a second time.

A breakfast of pancakes and tea used up the last of the

white gas. Fortunately I had a small kerosene heater and four gallons of fuel (intended as a heat source) that could serve to melt snow for drinking water and possibly for cooking. The dying hiss of the stove gave way to a faint, trumpetlike sound. As it became louder, I recognized the call of sandhill cranes, forced so low by the weather that they were barely able to clear the tips of the stunted trees on the ridge where the tent was pitched. Their six-foot wingspans, long straight necks, and purple-gray plumage gave them an almost surreal appearance. To have even one glimpse of them so close was more than an even trade for a missed meal at the lodge and a warm bunk in the old cabin. It occurred to me how little I really knew of their behavior. Where did they nest? Was it in the sweep and stretch of the grassy flats just west of Farewell ridge? What did they feed on? Berries? Insects? Seeds? Did they, like emperor geese, mate for life?

Aside from watching the cranes, there wasn't much to do but clear snow from the tent and eat, though when I tried to fry pancakes on top of the kerosene heater the results were anemic, doughy discs. A makeshift oven—one pot stacked inside another with an inverted skillet for a lid—and a few spoonfuls of Tang added to the batter met with more success. The cranes, meanwhile, continued to pass overhead, and each time they flew by I rushed outside for this rare, close-up view. A pattern developed: bake and eat a Tangcake, wash it down with tea, slip outside when the birds came by, and clear snow from the tent on my return.

The aftertaste of Tang and flour soon settled heavily on the back of my tongue. I was trying to wash it away with my third mug of tea when I heard the cranes again, but this time they sounded a lot more like a dinner bell.

De Montbel's determination to take only a Boone and Crocket-sized moose had resulted in no shots being fired, and no sustenance in the form of fresh meat. I longed to lift the lid on a Dutch oven filled with tender ribs and onions, the unctuous steam rising up to slick my cheeks and forehead. My father, after twelve years of successful hunts, once failed to get his moose. That was the year that mountain goat, black bear, and caribou filled our freezer. I was born to game meat, and I craved its smell, taste, and energy.

Grabbing my rifle, I climbed out of the tent. As the cranes drew near, I fixed my sights on the lead bird, but just before squeezing the trigger, I stopped and watched them disappear into the blizzard.

Back in the tent that evening, I started thinking about why I hadn't fired. My isolated circumstances and proximity to the birds had turned my relationship with them from casual to intimate. I also knew that although the hunting season was open, the regulations called for the use of a shotgun, not a rifle. That, of course, was a safety precaution, but here—where there were no people for miles—flying bullets were hardly a concern. And there was a clause in the regulations that allowed for the emergency taking of game for food. Certainly, an emergency begins long before one is falling down in the snow exhausted—but when? It seemed a simple thing to say, "Yes, it's okay to shoot one bird to eat," but I fell asleep wrestling with this conflict.

By morning, I put the cranes' fate in the hands of the weather: If it was still snowing when I stepped out, I would shoot the first bird within range. It was still snowing, but for the first time a low ceiling could be detected just above the tops of the tallest trees. Shortly, a small flock appeared.

Positioning myself on the ridge, I confidently swung my rifle and fired. Astonished, I watched them all continue without so much as a ripple in the clean lines they cut through the sky. I fired again with the same result. I suddenly felt embarrassed—not so much for having missed, but for having tried.

The snowfall slackened during the day, and the ceiling slowly lifted. At dusk, there were only occasional flurries as I pushed my way through the heavy snow to the airstrip. Even with a shovel it would have taken me at least two days to clear an area to land. The best Stan could do now would be to drop me supplies or a note telling me to wait it out. Earlier in the season, we had set up a small tent on the river below. Maybe at the lower elevation, I thought, the lesser accumulation of snow wouldn't be a problem for the airplane's big tires. It was a long trek but when I remembered the candy bars cached in the tent, my sweet tooth tipped the scales in favor of the hike. I slept better knowing I had a plan.

The morning dawned clear and while organizing my gear I kept looking to the west, expecting any minute to see the Piper headed my way. If Stan didn't appear by 11 a.m., I decided, I would start for the lower camp. At 10:45 everything was packed except my sleeping bag. The radio sat conspicuously in the corner of the tent—$2,000 worth of electronics. The extra ten pounds seemed manageable, and after some shuffling, it fit squarely on top of my load. At one minute past the hour I stuffed my sleeping bag and strapped it to my pack. The snow was well past my knees and so heavy and wet that it pressed obstinately against my legs. Experience had taught me that without snowshoes, hip boots were the best footgear for these conditions. Although they kept wool pants dry, they provided no flotation and little warmth. After stomping out a big arrow in the snow indicating my direction of travel, I headed off.

After being confined for so long it felt good to be moving again, but I hadn't gone far when the pack straps began cutting into my shoulders. I immediately regretted taking the radio, but retracing my steps uphill held no appeal. Under normal fall conditions, this trip would take a little over an hour—it would take me almost three.

When I finally reached the river I gratefully set down my pack and took drink after drink of the clear water, then glanced over to where the tent was supposed to be. Nothing. I saw only a small rise in the snow between two willows. Digging with my gloved hands I uncovered the tent and found an old coffee can containing six candy bars. I devoured three on the spot—the others took up residence in my pack.

My hopes rose when I heard the low putter of the Super Cub. Stan dipped his wings and began circling above me, but it was unclear if he wanted something from me or if he was merely planning his next course of action. Then it occurred to me that I should let him know what the snow depth was. As the plane droned above, I duck-walked through the snow, shaping a wide "20" with my thin rubber soles, wondering if the crude numbers would be decipherable from the air. Stan dipped his wings again but continued circling. Baffled, I watched the plane assume a straight course in the general direction of the lodge, as if departing. Then it banked sharply and headed directly toward me. A small plastic bag with a long piece of orange surveyor's tape attached fluttered down and landed nearby. I waded over, ripped open the bag and read: "Steve, the snow is too deep to land. Walk down to the South Fork. Maybe I can find a place there to pick you up. Stan."

As he came back around, I held up the surveyor's tape to confirm that I had located the airdrop. Alone again, I suddenly felt weak. Maybe it was just the downslide from my recent sugar fix, or maybe it was the note. What I had expected to read I couldn't say, but that clearly was not it. I pulled out my water bottle and sipped and stared up and down the river. The water flowed past, a gurgle and splash at my feet. Something in those liquid syllables was inspiring, and I felt my strength slowly return. Fortunately, I had no idea how far I had yet to travel. Miles we count off on a map or calculate as we fly over them are often surprisingly deceptive—mere numbers that never seem to account for all the twists and turns along the way.

Strapping on my pack, I had the impression it wasn't as heavy as when I had taken it off forty minutes before. That illusion of lightness was soon supplanted, however, by the pack's unrelenting shoulder straps cutting into my flesh. I again assumed a ponderous plod. My ten-pound rifle hung from a hook attached to the right side of the pack frame, causing extra strain on my shoulder and hip. Holding up the bottom of the frame allowed me to lift some of the weight off my shoulders and provided temporary relief.

My mind slowly disengaged from the rhythmic motion of my feet beneath the snow. I had, in a sense, already returned to the lodge; back to a cohesive group of hardworking, friendly people; to hot showers, a warm cabin, and incredible meals heavy with German influence—second and third helpings plus dessert; to a place where I was simply a guide and people more qualified than me would fill the roles of cook, dishwasher, menu planner, and evening storyteller.

My trance was abruptly shattered by a noise from the opposite bank of the river, and the world was instantly reduced to one image: a tawny, sleek-coated grizzly only sixty feet away. The bear's head-down posture and fixed gaze indicated a challenge. I immediately felt reduced to prey.

I carefully unhooked the rifle from my pack and worked the bolt. "Get out of here!" I yelled. In response, the bear, as if released from a catapult, jumped into the river and headed straight toward me. The incredulity of the moment was overwhelming and a gallery of inner voices started shouting instructions and questions:

Can this really be happening?

You don't have time to take your pack off.

Get down on one knee and steady yourself.

Shoot! Now!

Maybe it's bluffing?

Shoot!

A farcical play developed. From the wings I listened to an absurdly reasonable voice point out the inconvenience of killing the bear.

"You know you will have to take time to skin it. You will lose any chance you had of making the lodge today. You'll have to hike back for the hide and skull. The state will make you fill out piles of paperwork. Your hands will be very cold."

"Fire a warning shot."

When the bear was halfway across the shallow river, I raised the rifle sights above its head and fired. The bear continued straight toward me. Not a flinch, not a sign of altering its course. There was scarcely a second to make a decision.

I worked the bolt and drew an imaginary line in the snow on my side of the river. The debate was over—one toe across that line and the next shot would be aimed at its chest. The bear ran quickly up the steep bank and stopped. It made a loud "woof" and I tried unsuccessfully to keep the sights trained on the middle of its chest. The heavy pack was throwing off my balance and causing the rifle to sway in my hands. In the calmest voice I could muster I told the bear that I didn't want to kill it. It "woofed" again but didn't move forward. I went on talking.

"You don't want to be a rug."

"Why don't you just wander off and leave me alone?"

The grizzly gave a short, deep cough and quartered away. It stopped and glared several times, apparently reconsidering its retreat, as I continued talking. Finally, it slipped out of sight behind a stand of willows. With a deep breath, I reached in my pack for extra ammunition. Drawing open the bolt I stared in disbelief at an empty rifle! It took a minute to register. I hadn't replaced the two rounds fired at the sandhill cranes. The warning shot fired over the bear's head had been my last. As quickly as my fumbling fingers would allow, I crammed three cartridges in my rifle, my eyes rapidly searching the willow thickets for any sign of movement. The bear had plenty of opportunity for a surprise attack from the snow-covered bushes along both banks of the river. After reloading, I felt less confident than I had only moments earlier behind the assumed protection of an empty rifle. Fatigue vanished. The surrounding brush felt electric. No longer aware of my pack, sore shoulders, or heavy feet, I wanted only to be far, far away. I moved with a combination of speed and caution that was skewed well in favor of haste.

It wasn't until I reached the south fork of the Kuskokwim near the spot Stan thought he might be able to pick me up that I returned my rifle to its hook on the pack frame. Only then did I notice that the snow was significantly less deep at this elevation.

My anxiety slowly faded. Before me lay a mile and a half of braided river flowing around gravel washes and islands of willow, running low and clear with the cool weather. I worked my way across the first shallow channel to inspect a clearing as a possible landing strip. Almost four hundred feet long, it was plenty of runway, wide and flat, but the tall willows at each end were a problem. I forded the next patch of water, looking for a better site. Although the ultimate decision of whether to land would be Stan's, the responsibility of choosing a landing place was not one I took lightly. Each promising spot was rejected for one reason or another until I found myself more than halfway across the flat. Under normal water conditions I would never have made it this far without the risk of being swept away. Then the idea came to me that it might be possible to ford the main channel.

Eyes drawn to the spruce-covered slope rising on the other side of the river, I knew that once among those trees it would be a simple twenty-minute hike up the trail to the lodge. I imagined myself walking up, leaning my pack against the weathered logs, and opening the door to ask, "Am I late for dinner?"

The river was too deep along the edge of the main channel, but it fanned out in a series of riffles upstream, allowing a diagonal crossing. The water burbled and eddied around my legs with invigorating coolness. Like the creeks and rivers upstream, the tributaries of my past experience merged and pressed around me. There was the kit beaver laboring up the shallow May rapids of the Rohn. Bison calves red against the stone washes of the Post. The wreckage of a Cessna furrowing its way into the rubblestone of the upper Dalzell. Golden fin Dolly Varden hiding in the spring-fed runnels of the Hartman.

Then I heard Stan. I waved limply as he flew directly overhead. It was the first time I could remember the sight of that familiar airplane being so unwelcome. Not only was a ride now unnecessary, it was unwanted.

I turned to watch him fly on without any indication that he had seen me. I pressed on while he flew circles in the distance, searching in vain for my small image in the lengthening shadows.

As I traveled the well-worn trail, darkness began to fall. To my east, in the same twilight, a grizzly was leaving tracks, crisp and clean, wandering toward its denning site above the Dillinger River. In the same air, sandhill cranes were funneling through Mystic Pass on their way south, and I paused for a long moment, grateful for life, before descending the last slope to the lodge.

10

Something in the Bones

Strips of bacon were already laid out in neat rows in the cast-iron skillet as I pumped the Coleman stove with long, steady strokes. The yellow light of my headlamp was unnecessary for this rote procedure. I held a match to the burner and an orange flame erupted to life then turned blue.

The cold wood floor of the small cabin stung my toes through wool socks, as I stood absorbed in the pre-caffeine lassitude before dawn. I slipped into my flannel shirt, vest, and wool pants. It was late August. Stan had flown me into this mountain valley the day before. Our landing was as smooth as one could expect when a small airplane plants itself on the gravel surface of a pick-and-shovel-altered stream bank. Outside, the Alaska Range waited in the dark: unnamed peaks, clear mountain streams, an autumnal spectrum of color and wildlife in every direction. By 6:30 I would be heading into it, still sleepy but gradually awakening to the sights and sounds of the land.

Monte, the other guide in camp, remained motionless in his sleeping bag. His clients and my Swiss hunter, Rolf, were nestled away in two tents, separated from our crude cabin by dwarf birch and a narrow, willow-lined path. I wished the minutes could be stretched into hours. There was a stillness here that belonged to me. There were no decisions yet to be made, no judgments—just a new, unspoiled day.

It was a perfect morning, except for a stiffness of mind and body. I had had too little rest and my feet were bruised from weeks of sheep hunting. I never wanted to leave the comfort of my sleeping bag, especially those last few moments before my wristwatch alarm sounded. That's why I always prepared so well the night before—like a pilot with a preflight checklist—giving myself more time in the early hours. The bacon was in the skillet, the coffee pot ready to slide over the heat, the dishes done, the wood box filled. I had made sandwiches and placed them inside my pack, filled the water bucket, and scribbled a few lines in my journal before going to sleep.

I didn't like sharing camp with another guide. It made me feel claustrophobic. Monte and I had flipped a coin for the choice of direction the next day. He chose the preferred downstream valley. I would head up Dalzell Creek with Rolf. It looked like a nice day for a hike, even though I'd been told that the drainage led to a blind canyon that had never been known as a hangout for Dall rams. But experience told me never to discount surprises.

At first light Rolf and I worked our way up deeply rutted game trails, laying our tracks in those of moose, grizzly, black bear, and caribou. We crisscrossed the knee-deep, clear water many times, seeking the best walking. Rolf didn't say much. I hadn't asked him yet what part of Switzerland he was from or how the Alps compared with the mountains surrounding us. I had listened often enough to other Europeans. Their replies were much the same: *The mountains, they are beautiful too, just like this, though always there are people. Everywhere.* They would point across the valley like a teacher aiming at a wide blackboard. *Twelve people would be climbing that ridge, and there seven more, and there a family having a picnic, and there* . . . Then they would shake their heads and take a deep breath as their gaze swept across the scene before them.

We moved carefully into the mountains pausing often to train binoculars on the new vistas revealed by each step. In my years guiding, I had learned that most of the time it is better to climb high and look down, rather than hunt from the valley floor, but this was one of those places where broken ridges or steep faces limit travel.

A multicolored wave of bovine-shaped backs burst out of a small ravine and separated into four distinct bodies. The caribou moved in a fashion somehow graceful and awkward at once, a barrel-chested, spindly-legged glide-run. Their large, concave hooves clattered across a gravel bar, adding a backbeat to the faint clicking of their leg joints. They splashed through the stream kicking up spray, then tossed their heads, grunted, and disappeared.

Suddenly I felt that by losing the previous night's coin toss, I had really won. Caribou did that to me, but it wasn't just caribou. It could have been almost any animal or bird, or just the sun's rays cutting through thin clouds at exactly the right moment. I was thrilled to think that we were heading to a place I'd never been before.

French aviator Antoine de Saint-Exupéry thought that only the unknown frightens men. That is only part of the story. Though that which lies ahead, wrapped in clouds or hidden by the curve of a rock-strewn drainage, may spawn a multitude of phobias, more often than not it is what excites us. The undiscovered, both minute and grand, draws us with its magnetism. Perhaps the greatest confidence to press on comes when retreat is easiest, when we can simply pivot on the ball of a foot and follow the valley back to camp. Then it is natural to push onward, just a bit farther.

As we ascended, the creek shrank in size, its ankle-deep water cutting a lazy S-shaped path. Cautiously, we crept from rocky outcrop to cut bank. There was no wind, and the sun soon illuminated and warmed the valley.

High above us something shone brightly, a silver-white form distorted by the reflection of the sun's rays. I knew instantly what it wasn't: a sheep or an animal of any sort. Had other hunters climbed over the top from the far ridge and set up a plastic sheet shelter as a bivouac? The shiny object sat on a steep, exposed slope, a poor choice for a campsite. With my binoculars I could make out random shapes scattered about the area.

Stepping out of the sparse protection that the creek bed offered, we moved upward. On a gray-green slope half a mile distant stood thirteen ewes and lambs. We welcomed the chance to watch them while we caught our breath, but then renewed our ascent. We saw a flash of movement.

Whether it is the diamond-shaped markings—golden against dark, dense fur—or the slightly skewed lope of the thick, low-slung body that makes a wolverine difficult to confuse with any other animal, I am not sure. It angled down the mountain from the direction of the bright spot we were climbing toward, then without altering its gait or course it passed us and disappeared into the valley bottom.

By the time we reached the first patches of snow, the sun's glare had shifted, revealing the vertical stabilizer of an airplane. I recognized it immediately as a crash site. Part of me wanted to sprint ahead to inspect; the other part needed time to adjust to such a discovery. It seemed incredible that there could be an undiscovered wreck this close to the pass. No one had ever mentioned it to me, and I realized it could be days or decades old.

When we reached the first passenger seat I was surprised that the metal rails and side hinges were intact, the fabric unabused. It was as if someone had set it down on the spot and a light wind had nudged it over onto its side. We came across a second, then a third seat, spread out like trail markers holding some cryptic message. We paused at each one. I recognized the seats as the type used on single-engine Cessnas, exactly like those I had strapped into many times.

Scattered across the slope were cans of Olympia beer, faded from exposure to snow and sun. I studied the labels with the familiar image of the upside-down horseshoe. I remembered a TV commercial I'd seen years before. A man opens a can of Oly and begins drinking. A slow rotation, and the horseshoe settles into the proper position: luck will not drain out when the ends are up. Some of the cans were dented and drained, others sloshed with beer. Wouldn't the thin aluminum have burst when subjected to a winter's freeze? The condition of the seats suggested a recent crash, but the evidence of the beer was ambiguous.

I tried to recall the relationship of momentum to mass and velocity but my brief exposure to the study of physics was soon lost in an image of seats cartwheeling through space, each headrest proscribing an elliptical orbit around an invisible axis, the springs, padding, and seatback pouch all in a swirl of motion. I began to look around in earnest, thinking, for the first time, we might actually find some*body*.

And what about the wolverine?

Wolverines will eat almost anything, from berries to carrion. Though they feed on animals such as voles, squirrels, snowshoe hares, and birds, and occasionally kill moose, caribou, and sheep, they are better adapted for scavenging. They move constantly within their extensive home ranges, revisiting at times the sites of previous meals. It seemed a ghoulish notion that one would have found nourishment at the site of an airplane wreck. Then I saw the bones.

Forward of the airplane's tail, beneath the twisted frame that once held windows, rested the curve of a spine. The human backbone was bent into a sphinx-like position. My eyes followed the bony arch down to its connection with the pelvis, which was mostly covered with burnt rubble. There was no flesh clinging to the bones. No blood. No clothing. The vertebrae, humerus, radius, and ulna gave the impression of fossils-in-the-making. The lower half of the skeleton seemed to have disappeared.

Downhill, about six or eight feet away, lay the skull. It was intact except for a small irregular hole near the top. I took photographs of the pilot's remains, of the mangled propeller lying to the side, of the wing flattened against the mountain. From the markings on the tail I recorded the company name and airplane identification number. *Galena Air Service N6405H.*

Rolf and I walked a short distance away and sat down. I pulled our lunches from my pack and we ate in silence. I thought about all the times I'd flown with Stan. His recent hints that I should learn to fly made me uncomfortable. I didn't think I had the ability, the coordination to land on those narrow, short patches of rock and gravel he called airstrips. The thing was, I liked flying as a passenger. It was exhilarating to swoop and soar in the hands of a master without the responsibility of control. When I rode with Stan in his Super Cub, I could see his broad shoulders settle against the padded seat as if tension were drawn out of his body the instant he fastened his seat belt.

Now spread around me were the torn and bent pieces that had once formed an airplane—hundreds of reminders for me to keep my feet on the ground. How long had the fire burned to gut the fuselage like it did? Was the pilot's head severed from his body on impact or did he scream in pain, feel the hot lick of flames and hear the fuel-fed crackle and hiss as the song of his own funeral pyre?

I chewed my lunch slowly and swallowed without tasting. The caribou roast sandwich churned in my belly as I tried to make sense of the tragedy. My thoughts drifted. I gave the pilot a story. I gave him a name.

Mark was in his mid-twenties with a newly acquired commercial pilot's license and just over a thousand hours of flying time. It wasn't enough experience to land a job with a major airline, so he moved to Alaska where airplanes are ubiquitous and pilots a-dime-a dozen. He accepted a job with low wages and long hours, based out of a bush village he had never heard of before.

One morning in late fall, just after the nights began to outstretch the days, Mark received his last assignment. Low stratus clouds clung to the glaciers near the upper Tonzona River as he slipped through the Alaska Range, then down the west fork of the Yentna River on his way to Merrill Field in Anchorage. After dropping off his passengers, he loaded the airplane.

From pilot reports and scattered weather observations along his return route, he knew the weather was deteriorating. To be safe, he chose to fly a little farther south on his return, through Rainy Pass.

Just past Shell Lake, where the Hayes River dumps into the Skwentna, he grew concerned. The clouds were almost down to the treetops. Mark flew a tight circle around the sandbar northeast of Porcupine Butte, thinking that he could return to this landing strip if the weather got worse. He pressed on. At Shirley Lake conditions improved, revealing the broad Ptarmigan River Valley beneath a flat overcast.

Rain streaked the windshield as he turned up the third valley on his right. A bead of water formed at the top of the doorframe. The droplet swelled like a tick, then fell at an oblique angle to splatter on his pant leg.

The visibility lowered. Mark pulled back on the throttle, adjusted the prop pitch and set the flaps at ten degrees. Abeam of the heart-shaped alpine lake that shared the name of the pass, he slowed even more. He increased the flaps to twenty degrees and gripped the yoke tighter.

He had memorized the zigzag path of the pass: right, left, right, left, right. In theory it was simple. Once he cleared the summit all he had to do was follow the stream downhill into the Kuskokwim drainage. Yet everything looked different from the last time, when he had flown through at six thousand feet, leisurely looking for sheep and signs of the Iditarod trail. Even an act as simple as following water became difficult for Mark when things around him turned to vapor.

He drifted through mist and fog, and a pervasive, unsettling gray. All he could see was the stone kaleidoscope of the mountain face racing past his wing tip. Moisture collected in the small of his back, in his palms.

His feet were light on the rudder pedals, like an unicyclist balancing on a rope. Because he was not a tall man, he leaned forward to peer over the dashboard and felt the harness press upon his shoulders. Mark dared not let go of his visual contact with the vertical, crumbling rock—could not, would not, turn away from it. When he noticed his compass swinging too far to the south he thought there must be a magnetic ore deposit nearby. It should have read north by then. He eased in more throttle.

The last turn he would attempt in his life would come as more of a reaction than a decision. Throttle in to its hilt. Yoke hard left. His foot heavy on the rudder petal.

Then, just as the force of a sudden stop pulled his guts into a knot, he heard the cacophony of the entire nose wheel assembly ripping from the airplane in the mountain's sure grip. All went black.

Kinetic energy spun the left wing in a pirouette and deposited it on a rubble of rock—a collapsed shell of itself. The Continental engine smoked and hissed its way, a steaming, hot-pistoned bowling ball, into the valley's core. A wisp of black smoke curled up into the cool fall air.

Do any of us have the right to make up another's story, to mold multiple possibilities into one composite tale? The drive to explain is strong, and when we most want to find answers we often give in to our own flights of imagination. Later, I would find out that the crash had occurred in September, but I never learned the pilot's name or much about him.

If flying can lead to the kind of carnage I found that day

on the mountain, should humans ever attempt to take wing? Were it possible to ask the young man left in the wreckage near Rainy Pass that question, I would. Perhaps he would have agreed with Alexander Chase, who wrote, "Lovers of air travel find it exhilarating to hang poised between the illusion of immortality and the fact of death." Would the young aviator have told me that the opportunity to visit that space, albeit briefly, was enough?

Learning to fly made me uneasy, but I did go on to earn my pilot's license. I fought back panic and tried to ignore an internal voice that kept chanting *no, no, no, I'm not ready,* when Bruce, my instructor, stepped out of the airplane for the first time and told me to solo. My six hours of time seemed inadequate. But there was no graceful exit, I was an Alaskan *man* after all, so I pushed the throttle forward and hoped for the best. I imagined the engine quitting, the sudden appearance of a rogue wind shear that would make me fall from the sky, or a blown tire that would send me careening toward the ditch on landing.

None of that happened. I completed my requisite number of takeoffs and landings and taxied to the parking area. I left the airport that day already anxious about my next flight and still questioning Bruce's confidence in my abilities. Bruce, of calm demeanor; Bruce, who had thousands of hours of flying time; Bruce, who died years later at the controls of a DC-6.

I kept at it even though my guts churned before every flight. During my first landing at a controlled airport, the stabilizer crank handle came off in my hand. Another time the seat broke in my Super Cub, and I fell backwards onto the knees of my passenger. When the gear of a friend's Cub I was riding in collapsed on a remote beach and the plane suffered propeller and wing damage, I still did not stop flying.

Was I brave? Probably not. I knew that flying had little to do with courage. Courage could not be had merely through hours of training and money enough to pay for it. All my life I'd operated on a sliding scale between caution and risk, never feeling comfortable jumping into the deep end of the pool yet eventually taking the plunge. Despite my fears, I knew that a life without adventure would be unsatisfying. I found myself alternately apprehensive and exhilarated, hesitant and bold. I wonder if flying isn't just a metaphor for life—that no matter what we do, something inside us seeks a very personal and often momentary symmetry, when lift equals weight. Something light as air, heavy as stone, deep within us, seeking balance.

I remember bending down one last time to look at the vertebrae. The bones that protect the spinal cord, the message path to the brain, have fins shaped like wings. Humans don't have hollow bones or feathers, but a spine which, in silhouette, seems ready to take flight.

Porcupine Pass

11

It is a warm afternoon in late August with no rain. We have climbed steadily all day up the main fork of Marta Creek, crossing and re-crossing the clear water. Now we move along a ridge, pausing to catch our breath and glass for sheep. My client walks well and talks little, and it is good to be in the mountains with him.

At the highest point of ascent our eyes trace the contours of the upper reaches of the Jones River. Gray, steep slopes dominate the scene. The Jones is a silver thread at the bottom, visible at one curve, disappearing at the next. There is less vegetation than in most other small drainages in the Teocalli Mountains, mostly scree slopes and barren ridges. Relaxed, we begin descending downslope from the notch. Despite the lack of any sightings, this is sheep country, and we keep watch for white dots on the crags. But my mind drifts. I am absorbed in the pleasure of losing altitude easily. The tip of my walking stick softly spears the earth with the rhythm of my stride.

I see an ursine sway below us. My client barely misses colliding with me as I stop suddenly and raise my binoculars. The contours of the mountain hide half of the animal's bulk, as if it were walking in a ditch. The animal is brownish black, silhouetted by yellow-tipped guard hairs. I focus the binoculars with the tips of my fingers. A porcupine. I see now how one could mistake it for a bear. When the perspective of size is gone, the similarity in color and movement is surprising.

Plodding directly toward us, the porky moves up and down without seeming to progress. How many hours has it been at this pace since it saw its last willow? I know it is miles away from any stand of aspen, birch, or spruce. I wonder if this prickly, twenty-five pound rodent is on a pilgrimage to some spruce cambium Mecca or just more solitary than others. Breeding season is not for another three months. It must be another urge. As we watch him my admiration grows. I've never seen a porcupine at such high elevation.

Then suddenly I realize that soon he will see us and probably become frightened and turn to descend. I crouch down and motion the hunter to follow. We stay low and move off to the side to let him pass. The porcupine, catching a glimpse of movement, momentarily turns his wire brush of a body toward the valley. I curse under my breath and wonder why I want so much for this animal to reach his goal, whatever it may be. Perhaps I want in some way to apologize to the three or four porkies I have struck dead with an axe or shovel.

A sharp blow on the snout is all it takes to kill a porky. Its body relaxes, its eyes grows dim. That's what I'd read, and it seemed simple, poetic somehow: a passing of grace, a clean transport into the afterworld. Until I tried it. It was not beautiful or easy; it took multiple blows, each a more brutal thud into a softening skull. A shudder ran through the bristled body and the claws of its front feet raked the air in one last effort to escape.

In hunting camp, I always tried to drive the porcupines off first, away from the plywood they devoured for the taste of glue, away from the antlers and horns they are known to chew. Too often they returned, usually at two or three in the morning. I would stumble out of my bunk, flashlight in one hand, shovel or stick in the other. I gave them three chances to wander on, herding them away from camp, but it was a precious five hours of sleep interrupted. It was a tired and frustrated man who lashed out and ended their lives.

Porcupines are not benign creatures of the forest; they often leave destruction in their wake. During winter cold snaps they may spend days or weeks in one tree, methodically stripping away the bark, feeding on the inner layer. They chew on axe, hoe, or shovel handles, anything salt-impregnated through people's handling.

My neighbor used to tell the story of a coyote, emaciated, unable to eat, its mouth a pincushion-snout-full of festering agony. He knew this because he considered coyotes "varmints" and shot every one he saw. Humans have a long list of open-season, no-limit pests, depending on the year, the geography, people's interests and moods: squirrels, shrews, voles, magpies, gray jays, sparrows that eat garden seedlings, or the black bear that preys on moose calves. We have put bounties, at one time or another, on bald eagles, coyotes, wolves, and even Dolly Varden.

If backed into a corner or threatened, a porky raises its quills, presents its bristling back, and lashes its tail back and forth. The vigorous flipping of this appendage adds force to drive quills into an attacker. But it uses this technique in self-defense, the same justification *Homo sapiens* often use for violence.

After a brief pause the porcupine resumes its upward

course over dull-white leaf lichen and alpine bearberry. It is odd that this small mammal causes remorse in me, when my purpose in the mountains is to help someone kill a sheep.

As my hunter and I descend the slope, I turn to look at the porcupine one last time. He is a brown speck in this alpine panorama, climbing toward the pass. He is not in any hurry. He is a resident of these mountains and valleys, while I spend only two or three months at a time here.

The log cabin we will return to when we quit the mountains has been around only a little over twenty years. It was hastily built of unpeeled spruce, the crude notches requiring new moss chinking each year. The first hunting season came on too fast and a canvas roof was thrown up. The light came through, adding a cheery glow to the bunks, log table, and Blazo box kitchen counter. Wolverines, bears, and porcupines found easy access through the thin cloth. A log and sod roof eventually replaced the canvas, but it didn't always keep out the critters. And why should it?

The porcupine is higher now. Soon he will be over the rise and making his way down to the west fork of the river. If he follows the river's clockwise course he will eventually be in the valley floor, heading northwest. He will arrive at the cabin. Whether he lingers or not doesn't matter. By then I'll be gone, departed like the sandhill cranes until the next season.

12

Trespass

I stumbled into camp at 1 a.m. Returning from an isolated Alaska Peninsula valley with my hunter and laden with a heavy bear hide, I was thinking my work was finished and I could sleep late the following morning. Scott, my fellow guide, and his hunter, Eric, were in a somber mood. Scott, ever the stoic Swede, was more subdued than usual as he congratulated us.

There was an unspoken rivalry between Scott and me. It was friendly and tempered with mutual respect, but I knew the feeling of satisfaction whenever I returned with a trophy larger than Scott's. He must have known similar emotions when the roles were reversed, but I always thought of us as teammates, not adversaries, so I was surprised at the glum reaction to our day's success.

I sipped a beer while Scott reheated stew and laid out bread and butter. Over the hiss of the gas stove, Scott said that Eric had also shot a bear. He spoke quietly, offering a brief recap of the day. Scott and Eric had spotted two mature bears traveling together. After hours of observing and stalking, Eric shot one of them, which ran into an alder patch and died. The second bear refused to leave, and attempts to scare it away succeeded only in using up the remaining daylight, so the hunters returned to camp.

It was late, I was tired, and I couldn't figure out a way of shirking my duty, of not doing everything I could to help. I felt bound by our friendship and our shared responsibility as guides to complete the job and collect the trophy as safely as possible. Before the last swallow of watery ale slid down my throat, I announced I would join them at first light. Nestled in my sleeping bag, staring at the canvas ceiling, I hoped one night's passing would solve this problem—that the guardian bear would vanish by morning and we could simply slip in and finish our business.

We weren't so lucky.

As we approached the area the next morning, our view of the bears was from the bank of a small stream, through an opening crosshatched with alder branches still thick with the dying leaves of late October. We tried to drive the live bear away from the dead one by shouting, waving arms, and shooting into the cliff above its head. Despite explosions of rock and dust, the bear stared back at us with beady eyes, motionless one moment, then pacing in quick, jerky movements as if tethered or caged.

We decided to assault the bruin's most acute sense: smell. The human scent is an odor bears often run from. But there was a problem. With a move upwind we would lose sight of the bear and not know if it had fled, followed us, or continued its vigil. I considered volunteering to go upwind alone, so Scott and Eric could observe the bear's reaction, but the tall grass and thick brush that would instantly swallow me from view was intimidating. The idea of three loaded rifles in our experienced yet anxious hands, when we didn't know exactly where each of us was, gave me the willies.

Together we shouldered our way through the thicket along the upstream bank, turned left, crossed the water, continued a hundred yards, and stopped. Hemmed in by dense foliage, we stood with the wind at our backs. I imagined our smell, that *other animal* stench wafting toward the bear in wisps and curls. I had no idea how long it would take to spoil an area with our odor.

Twenty or thirty minutes passed before we carefully followed our tracks back to the vantage point on the bank of the stream. Only one lifeless form remained—the sentinel was gone. Its absence should have made me feel better, but it didn't. Although the live bear may have run off for good, it could also be a few yards back in the bushes, waiting or circling behind us.

Scott and I had two clients each this season. We'd taken four bears, and I didn't want to shoot another. Forcing the issue by going into the tight confines of the brush might lead to the killing of number five, but I couldn't walk away. An animal had been killed and the least, the absolute least, we could do was retrieve the hide. We headed into the alder patch.

Flecks of dirt appeared on the thin layer of snow. Alder branches were clawed and bitten, the earth trampled and scraped. It was a crisscrossed maze of claw and pad imprints: the helter-skelter impressions of an animal in the center of its own chaos.

I was the expert by default, based on my eight years guiding—four of those seasons exploring this remote valley. If Scott and Eric could have read my mind or known the uncertainty beneath my sweaty skin, they would have questioned following me into the thick tangle of brush in the first place. I would have gladly let them take the lead.

As we inched along through the mat of alders, I waited for a sense of calm command to flood through me, but it wasn't happening. I felt slow and thick. The crunch of snow underfoot increased steadily, matching the drumming in my ears. My right thumb rested on the rifle's safety. A glance back at Scott didn't ease my anxiety, but made me realize how much greater it would be if I was alone. Less than a hundred yards separated us from our destination, yet it felt much farther. I turned to the signs of the second bear's rage in front of me.

In the thick weave of brush it was impossible to focus on a single point. My eyes darted from the muskeg-mottled hump of the dead bear to the cat's cradle of branches—left, right, straight ahead, and back. I searched for movement or a patch of furry brown in the spaces between the myriad clumps of broad, oval leaves. It was too much to take in. I asked Scott to watch to the right and Eric to cover our back trail while I concentrated on what was happening in front and to the left.

Crouched, elbows splayed, feet spread wide for balance, the three of us moved slowly, like soldiers patrolling a danger zone. There was an intensity and comradeship between us, and I knew what combat troops must feel. That connection pulled us forward, rifle barrels pushing aside branches, index fingers hovering on triggers, until we stood beside the dead bear.

It lay in a freshly dug, moist depression with dirt and moss piled on its belly. The head and legs stuck out from the tortoise shell-shaped mound in a hasty and incomplete burial.

Eric stood guard while Scott and I quickly scooped and brushed away the mixture of soil and torn vegetation. As the last layer was removed, my eyes locked on a narrow strip of red flesh between the bear's hind legs. The sight was eerie and unnerving—the genitals were missing. Scott must have seen it. Eric too. No one commented.

I reached over, grabbed my rifle, and stood. I had a vision of skinning the bear: a blade's keen edge rolling dense, oily fat before it. A knife stroke, a quick glance up, a stroke, then suddenly out of the bushes, a charge.

We have to get out of the alders, I thought.

The situation called for a quick plan. We decided to roll the bear into the stream and float it down to a place with more elbowroom. Feverishly, we sawed off alders that blocked our way. Our fingers slid deep into the musky hair and tightened to fists, as we bent low and leaned into the body. We pushed hard and the bulk rolled a few feet closer to the water. Heads up, we quickly scanned the area, shifted our rifles back to within arms' reach, and dug in for another try. The mass turned grudgingly.

With one final shove the bear slid into the stream with a heavy splash. We jumped in after it and guided the body around two, three, four bends. At the edge of a tiny sandbar, Scott and I skinned the bear—a sow—while Eric stood, rifle ready, at the bank's crest. When we finished, we lashed the hide and skull on our backs and started the slow pack back to camp.

I don't remember if I thought about burial, guardianship, or bonds between animals on that walk. But questions that still trouble me were spawned on the trail that day in late October. I knew this much: when a bear buries something, it is an assertion of ownership. Normally it is to cache food.

I had seen plenty of moose, caribou, and even sheep claimed by bears for that purpose.

I knew, too, that brown bears cannibalize. A veteran guide once told me that brown bears rarely eat others bigger than themselves. He told me they could "smell the size," and if they happened on a dead bear, they respected that smell by not eating it for days, maybe weeks, until the odor of decaying flesh left no trace of the bear's original and individual odor.

Anecdotes from old-timers are often a mix of knowledge derived from observation and a desire to impress an audience. What would the old guide have thought of this burial and the parts of the bear that were consumed? Perhaps, as a biologist later suggested, the bear was not targeting specific body parts, but just starting to eat opportunistically when we disturbed its feeding. The same biologist had not heard of anything like it and admitted the story was strange.

The biologist's explanation was reasonable and educated, but ultimately it was a guess. For me at least, the bears' relationship to one another mattered. The guardian bear was bigger, slightly darker, and I guessed it was a boar. But mature bears are more likely to travel together during the spring mating season and generally don't form lasting ties. If they weren't one-time mates, then what were they? Siblings? Or even a closer bloodline, a sow and grown cub?

The sow's teeth were chipped and worn, and when we skinned her we found an old, healed, small-caliber bullet wound in the shoulder muscles. I wondered if the instinct for a sow to protect her cubs could be reversed. Could a cub, more sensitive than most, assume a role as guardian for its wounded mother? Perhaps an internal compass could steer a young bruin to years of nurturing instead of following a more conventional path of going alone after it matured. Or had we run across a sexual deviant of the beast world—a twisted *Ursus arctos* with an Oedipus complex?

Why do my memories of that morning remain unsettled? Being in a state of hyperawareness, dreading each step forward, the mind is liable to magnify anything abnormal. Maybe I blew the significance of the mutilation out of proportion because circumstances had gone beyond my comfort zone—past my preconceived ideas of the interior lives of animals—into an issue of privacy or even voyeurism.

There can, of course, be a trap in viewing other species in human terms. Whatever the bears' relationship, something was operating between them that I can never really fathom. I can't shake the feeling we crossed a line that day well beyond the killing game.

The uneasiness lingers: I remember the blood-red wound, the skinned carcass; the sound of the guardian bear's feet crunching the frozen ground, and its small, fierce eyes.

13

Ruse of Rocks

As I step into the fog with my hunter close behind me, even the rocks settling beneath my feet are hushed. My nose, the back of my hand where my grip tightens on my walking stick, the lobes of my ears exposed below my woolen cap, are interfaces of warm body and cool air. Moisture forms thick, sweet droplets about my mustache and lips, and I can tell from glancing at my slick knuckles that my cheeks glisten too. The ridge we're ascending is no longer one shoulder of a prominent peak in the Teocalli Mountains; it's now a sloped wall of rock looming before our faces, veiled at its margins.

But I'm not concerned. I've traced this route many times from high ridges on the opposite side of the drainage. There are no false turns, just a steep spine leading to a bowl where I've seen sheep on a number of occasions, their sturdy necks bent down, chewing on tufts of bunch grass. In this section of the Alaska Range, when the early morning fog blankets the mountains, I no longer consider taking a day of rest. In the afternoon, somewhere in a notch high among the crags, the stillness will lose its hold and slip away with a persistent alpine breeze. I've sat often enough on a valley floor looking up, mocked by sheep trails cut hard into the scree, by a cirque lake or a hanging valley too distant to explore so late in the day. So now I don't wait for the sun's emergence but climb to greet it.

The moment I enter this damp, white world, the tether

that holds me to duty is loosened. My mind drifts. I am no longer a hunting guide.

I am the lead climber on the final slope to the summit of Aconcagua, gaining strength with every breath. I am the sole survivor of the Franklin expedition about to be feted. I am Shackleton. I am Hillary. I am Messner and Mawson and Scott. I speak twenty-nine languages, am a champion swordsman, and tonight have a date with Virginia, owner of the smile I watched sweeten from the third grade until high school graduation. She leans into me and gently squeezes my arm. I look down in search of delicate fingers to find the loden-gloved hand of my hunter. He wants to know what we will do if the fog does not lift. "We'll see," I answer, thinking that is exactly what we won't do.

The climb is easier now, but the fog is thicker. I lean into it as if it has a slope of its own. If we veer slightly to the left we should enter the bowl, but can I find the ridge again? A few steps and I look back. Okay from here. A few steps more and I'm not so sure. I begin to wonder if I should turn back but notice a rock larger than the others with a distinct patch of moss on the top. "Mossy rock, mossy rock," I say to myself and step forward. The next rock looks like a sleeping turtle, and beyond that there is one with a flat top. Flattop, Turtle, Moss. Those two ahead, nearly identical, the Twins. Twins, Flattop, Turtle, Moss—I'm feeling clever. Until the next rock looks a lot like—a turtle.

But this rock is larger than the first. Big Turtle, Little Turtle? Now I'm not so sure if the first one looked like a turtle at all. Why didn't I study it more? Maybe this mountain is scattered with turtlish boulders. The way back from here is easy: Twins, Flattop, Turtle, Moss—or is it Turtle, Flattop, Moss? We sit down.

Looking up, I make out the deep, blocky chest of a ram, facing left, bedded down. "A sheep." My nose almost touches my hunter's ear as I speak. "We'll wait here." He stares into the belly of the cloud, then glances at me with eyebrows slightly arched—the look of someone who has faith but has yet to see the vision. The world swirls and blurs. We slip behind Big Turtle. When the fog clears out we will need the cover of this rock.

Less than a hundred yards away the sheep lies motionless. The mass of the ram's chest tells it's a mature animal. But is it a trophy? I search for a hint of honey-colored horns. When the sheep is finally visible there will be little time to judge the horns' length, depth, width, the size of the bases, the symmetry.

My hunter shivers as he fastens the flaps of his cap beneath his chin, buttons his collar tightly around his neck. Quietly he pulls his knees to his chest and rubs his legs. I stare at the fuzzy form before us until my eyes water. There is an odd angularity to the outline, too much geometry. I hold my breath when I feel the breeze on my damp face. The weather's about to break. A glimpse of ridge here, rubble there. Patches of clarity slowly emerge, bringing into focus more and more of our surroundings. Then there it is before me. Not a hundred yards away, but twenty feet. Motionless. An outcropping of quartz, no larger than a shoebox.

I stand up cold and stiff, the only sheepish animal on this mountain, and start for the ridge. I look down as we walk and notice that each boulder we pass looks very much like a boulder and holds little distinction from the rest.

14

Almost Too Legal

It was a parable that Stan Frost liked to tell. One of his young guides allowed a client to shoot a small brown bear. Once back at camp, the thought of ridicule heaped upon the client by hunting buddies back home for returning with such an unimpressive trophy made the wealthy hunter squirm. He pulled a huge roll of one hundred dollar bills from his pocket and methodically placed one crisp bill after another in front of Stan. He wanted to bury the bear and go out and get a bigger one. "How much would it take?" he asked as he continued to lay down the greenbacks.

"Well, let's see," Stan began. "If we get caught, you would have to cover the fine and court costs. Of course if they confiscated my airplane, I would need a new one." The bills left the hunter's hand more slowly, but continued to pile up as Stan drew on his pipe, "They would revoke my guide license and take away my areas. I would need to be able to provide for my family in the custom to which we have become familiar—say for five years—until I could establish a new career." With a *harrumph* the hunter grabbed the money from the table, shoved it deep into his pocket, and left the tent.

I guided for Stan for over a decade and although he displayed respect for the wildlife, I can't say he never contemplated manipulating the regulations' gray areas. He began guiding in a time when there were more freedoms, fewer watchful eyes. Years later he admitted that my eagerness to comply with the regulations, though irritating, helped keep him on a straighter path.

But following rules, I was to learn, was not always the most prudent course of action. One September day after the last client had departed, I wandered into Farewell Lake Lodge in the late morning to share my thoughts with Stan on a building project, but Stan had other ideas. "Marta thinks we need more meat for the winter. I've had my spotting scope focused all morning on a bull moose halfway down the lake, so why don't I take the video camera, you grab your rifle, and we'll see what happens?"

The nearly empty meathouse and freezer had more to do with international economics than a lack of game. For years the deutsche mark-dollar exchange rate had been favorable for German clients, who constituted the majority of our hunters. Since Germans could not bring wild game meat back to Europe, we were the beneficiaries of their harvests. But now, by the mid-1980s, things had changed. Most of our hunters were domestic and took the bulk of their meat home.

"Stan," I said, "You don't get a chance to hunt anymore, why don't I take the video?"

"Oh no, that's all right."

"But really Stan, I don't mind at all!"

"No, Steve. I think you should grab your rifle."

Whether it was an eagerness to operate the video camera or reluctance to pull the trigger that we shared, I'm not sure. Stan could be diplomatic, playful, or blunt when dealing with his guides, but he was always boss. I shouldered my rifle.

Stan and I carefully worked our way through the black

spruce lining the shore of the lake. As we neared the spot he'd last seen the moose we stopped. Winds were picking up and beginning to swirl. Rather than spook the animal out of the area, we returned to the lodge. Before I snapped my tool belt around my waist, I asked Stan if I could look for the moose alone if the winds stabilized later and he was busy. He nodded.

Hours later, as I knelt at the shore of Farewell Lake to slake my thirst, whitecaps no longer dotted the water's surface. A glimpse of white flickered through the trees to the west. Antlers. I grabbed my rifle and binoculars from the bunkhouse and headed to the lodge.

The video camera sat on the downstairs counter. It was a two-unit affair, heavy and cumbersome. Long cords attached the camera to the deck and battery, which were carried in a padded case on a strap slung over the shoulder. I was drawn toward this new way of shooting. Though days off were rare, Stan had allowed me to take the camera on several occasions. I took footage of beavers dragging willows along the sloughs of the lower Jones River. I climbed up to a band of rams in a hard southeast blow. Along the trail to Tin Creek I captured the striped fan tail of a ruffed grouse on tape as the bird strutted about my feet.

I assumed Stan and Marta were in their living quarters above the kitchen. Maybe it was best not to disturb them, I told myself, in a feeble attempt to disguise my own selfishness. I wanted another turn at operating the video camera. I grabbed it and quietly headed up the lake.

The breeze was still in my favor, cooling the right side of my face as I stopped on a slight rise. The sound of waves lapping against the shore seemed to increase in volume—strange considering the dying wind—until I realized something was walking in the water. I crouched down and through a tunnel of branches saw a cow moose ankle-deep in the lake. She stopped, bent her hind legs slightly, and urinated. Removing the camera's lens cap, I focused on her dark outline silhouetted by the slate-blue lake.

Weeaahhhoowww. Her call carried clearly to my ears and into the camera's microphone. In a few strides she was gone from view. With a cow in the area, I figured the bull could not be far away.

With a dry, broken branch I flailed at a nearby tree, creating hollow thunks and raking sounds like antlers against wood. Silence. Then I cupped my hands to my mouth and sent a challenge into the forest with a low, guttural *ghluckk.*

Ghluucckkk, came an answer.

I saw a flash of white through the spruce—ivory-tipped points, swaying heavily, moving in my direction. I swung the camera to my shoulder and began shooting, twisting the focus ring to keep the image sharp. Now and then the bull disappeared into the folds of the boreal slope, but he kept coming. Seventy yards. Forty yards. He dipped into a small ravine.

Soon the bull emerged through a line of brush and stopped. I set the camera at my feet and shouldered my rifle. I'd had my fun, it was time to bring home the bacon. As the bull stepped into a small clearing I aimed for his neck and squeezed the trigger.

BOOM. He went down hard, as if thrown to the ground. With my rifle ready, I walked casually over to the moose. He lay, four legs uphill. His rack, almost five feet wide, pointed toward the lake. There was a slight tremor to his hooves, one last sign of life. I slipped the rifle's strap over my shoulder.

The hunting regulations state that a harvest ticket must be validated immediately upon taking game. I'd always suggested that my clients do this right away, before the joy of photos, the challenge of skinning, and the drudgery of packing made one forget to punch the ticket. I pulled my tag from my wallet and cut out the month with my hunting knife. As the little green triangle fell to the earth, I turned the ticket clockwise and located the date.

Then, from a dozen feet away came a loud grunt. In one quick movement the bull's four legs swung an arc high over his body. In an instant he was on his feet lunging toward me— eight brow tines and twelve points aimed at my chest.

Tearing the rifle from my shoulder, I stumbled backwards. As I fell away from the sweeping antlers, I shot from the hip at the brown blur. He turned hard left like a cutting horse and thundered in the opposite direction. Regaining my feet, I fired again.

Thwaacck, the sound of a solid hit.

As the moose collapsed I thought, "Oh no, that's where I laid down the video camera!" I envisioned small fragments of plastic, metal, and glass beneath nearly a ton of moose. Stan would not be pleased. I eased forward to find the video camera intact, just a few feet from the bull's nose. Despite the glazed look of his eyes, I prodded the moose with a stick to confirm that my last shot had finished him off. Looking him over, I found where the first bullet had hit high on the neck, just above the spine. That shot had sent a strong but temporary jolt through his nervous system. The second shot from the hip had only clipped a few hairs on the top of his neck.

Had I been skewered by the business end of the bull moose, help would have been slow to arrive. No one back at the lodge heard the shots. I imagined myself gored like a hapless matador, riding backwards on a bloody point of antler or lying on the muskeg with puncture wounds to the chest, a froth of blood on my lips.

Never would I have allowed a client to approach a downed animal in such a careless manner. A momentary lapse of caution. Caused by what? Complacency?

My neighbor, Howard Bowman, once told a newcomer to bush Alaska, "Everything here can kill you." That pretty much covers it. What makes the headlines are the powerful, the sharp, and the unpredictable: bears, avalanches, airplane crashes, boats capsizing.

We are surrounded by myriad possibilities for harm. We travel, literally, on thin ice. Static electricity can turn gas into flame. A chimney fire or a leaky propane tank can lead to disaster. We exist mostly in harmony with chainsaws, axes, and gaff hooks, but sometimes, a nick from the blade of a knife or the slight touch of chainsaw chain to boot leather can be a good thing, reminding us to pay attention. "To be alive at all involves some risk," wrote Harold MacMillian. Sure, and sometimes it doesn't pay to be in a hurry to punch your ticket.

15

Tracks on the Pingston

It was the first week of September, too early to be feeling such a bite to the air, an icy slap to nose, cheeks, and fingers that made my skin feel balloon thin. I looked down the short path that connected my campsite to the broad riverine flats sculpted by Pingston Creek. The creek's headwaters trickle down from near the boundary of Denali National Preserve in a meandering northwest path eventually adding a glacial snowmelt signature to the Tonzona River, then sweeping on to the Kuskokwim. Due to a dry autumn and the premature chill that locked precipitation in the mountains as snow, the creek's only channel now flowed low and clear along the west side of the draw.

I rubbed my hands together and slipped them into the pockets of my wool jacket. Maybe my resistance to the elements had ebbed from dealing with a recent client, a mercurial Quebecois whose moods ran hot and cold like a shower in a cheap motel. In a couple of days I would fly up to check on my last two hunters of the year who were situated at separate mountain camps with assistant guides. The season wasn't going badly—my guides were doing a fine job, my airplane was running well, and even the temperamental Canadian had departed in a jovial mood. So why was I worried?

If this cold snap ushered in snow, I was ill prepared. With only one round-nosed shovel, no preheater for my Super Cub, and no covers to put on the wings and tail, my guides and clients could easily be stranded if the snow became too deep. I hoped they were okay, not just because successful hunts are good for business. Accidents and misjudgments occur, sometimes in a flash. As a small-time outfitter, which included the roles of pilot and guide, I was the one to whom the entire burden shifted. I grabbed an armload of split spruce and shouldered my way back into the wall tent.

A stained mug sat on top of the wood stove. Coffee was my wilderness plasma, and I started each day with a transfusion. Although the first few cups took me from sleepy and stiff to attentive and agile, additional imbibing got me in trouble. When I stayed in camp I sometimes drank it all day. Caffeine made the whole of me, from hip boots to wool hat, flicker and hum with an internal charge. It also lubricated my anxious thoughts.

I finished the pot and headed outside. On the gravel bar runway I paced back and forth, pitching large and loose stones off to the side. It kept me warm but offered little relief from an assortment of vexations. I thought about the license fees I needed to remit to the state by the end of the year. I mulled over the dearth of clients booked for the following season, and the permits and contracts that made the guiding business increasingly akin to office work.

I was squandering valuable time, fretting then fretting about fretting. What I needed was a break from the concerns and responsibilities of my job. Surrounding me were trees, tundra, and quiet that I hardly noticed.

I decided to hike upriver.

Ambling up the valley, I followed a serpentine path around willow scrubs and dry washes. The Alaska Range spread left and right, though I caught only a tease of its rocky, white mass from my low-angled perspective.

The brisk air nipped my ear lobes and sliced at the exposed break of flesh between gloves and jacket cuffs. The tinkling rush of the creek came cleanly to my ears as exercise and cold air freeze-dried the caffeine from my system. My shoulders softened and my fist eased its grip on my walking stick.

As I often do when I am alone, not rushed, and miles from anywhere, I wondered what it would be like to live year-round in such a place. The stunted black spruce and tundra of the undulating foothills did little to slow the wind, though white spruce grew in scattered pockets along the margins of the creek. Most of these trees were crooked and severely tapered, but there were enough to build a modest cabin. At my feet, moose and bear tracks webbed the dirt and gravel surface. Caribou trails traced the ridges, and sheep ruminated and mated in the nearby mountains.

But there were drawbacks. Cut banks revealed poor, thin soil unsuitable for serious gardening. Fish were few and far between, and neighbors even farther. It was beautiful country in its own stark fashion but a recipe for a hardscrabble life.

In a depression of dried mud and sand between gravel bars, I noticed the four-toed, staggered tracks of a wolf. The lone animal had walked the creek bottom sometime since the August rains and before the September chill. The even spread of slightly splayed prints, hind and front tracks appearing almost as one, evidenced an unhurried pace. I looked up from the tracks to the mountains. An encounter five weeks and five miles removed from where I stood came flooding back.

At the end of July my wife Anne and I were preparing the camp on the Pingston. We joked that it was our "working honeymoon," coming just two weeks after our wedding. We cut firewood, cleared brush, bagged another outfitter's leftover trash, and set up a couple of wall tents. After several days' work, we decided to fly into the mountains to locate an old camp.

The site was overgrown with alders, but it was easy to spot from the air because of a friend's detailed directions. I made a low pass in order to inspect the gravel bar along the creek's edge, and then banked sharply, lined up into the breeze, and landed. We rolled to a stop and I killed the engine. The prop slowed and I opened the door.

Instantly the cockpit filled with another sound: howling. Precise and penetrating, it stunned us in our seats; the sound seemed to emanate from just beyond the wing tips. I'd heard wolves howl before, but never like this. Never so close. For a long moment, the steel tubing and fabric surrounding us disappeared, and we sat in a private concert hall.

After several minutes I whispered to Anne, "Let's get out." We unbuckled and slid to the ground. On the steep hillside above us, about one hundred yards away, a large gray wolf strode in measured steps. With no sign of hurry or alarm, the animal kept itself in our full view, acting like a decoy.

The howling became intermittent, with each long lament framed by an eerie silence. We couldn't see any other wolves; we only heard them echo up from the brush. Electricity charged the air.

The possibility that a den was near and that pups were being led away under cover of thick brush occurred to us. Later we figured out, based on the time of year, that it was a rendezvous site, a meeting place for the wolves: a post-den, pre-world staging area used between the time pups are weaned and when they begin to hunt with the rest of the pack. These pups at the end of July would have been about twelve weeks old and just beginning to travel along on hunts. They were not ready to join in the kill yet; that would come closer to the end of the year.

The surrounding sound experience may have been the best wedding present of all. I took it for a good omen. Anne cocked her head and smiled. The look on her face, the awe that we shared, gave me confidence in our future. We watched the wolf disappear around the curve of the hillside. The howling faded and stopped.

Anne was on the other side of the mountains now, in a small office, tutoring high school students. The recollection of our shared moment made me think of her with pleasure and longing.

A short distance from the wolf tracks I knelt at the creek's bank and ladled water to my lips with the palm of my hand. Sweet water, so cold it hurt my teeth.

All the things that had earlier been gnawing, rodent-like, at the edges of this fine day had vanished. I began the hike back to camp. The gravel passed easily under my boots in a hypnotic blur. Silently, I recited Robert Service verses, one after the other. My guiding-honed eyes methodically scanned the country before me.

A flash of gray-brown color stopped me in my tracks. Then I saw another glimpse of earth-toned movement, three hundred yards away to my left at the base of the steep-cut bank that defined the creek's edge.

Two wolves loped toward me. They had a youthful bounce

in their gait, a spring in their steps that lifted their thin-shouldered bodies effortlessly off the ground. I slipped behind a stand of willows and watched. They were pups of the year, maybe fifty pounds apiece, traveling side by side.

They hadn't spotted me. Instead they shot glances back and forth to each other in a *follow me—no, you follow me!* romp. They were covering ground fast, moving in my general direction. I looked down to see that a dry wash ran from where I stood to a point where I might intercept the wolves. I crawled into the natural ditch and kept my belly and butt low, scurrying.

A short howl echoed down from the top of the cut bank. I stopped and peeked at the pups' progress. Another low-toned, truncated howl came from the thick stand of black spruce at the bank's crest. The young wolves either didn't understand the warnings or chose to ignore them. They kept coming, and I scrambled along with elbows and ankles flying.

Reaching the end of my cover, out of breath, I halted. The wolves closed to within ten feet. Curious about their reaction to my presence, I stood to full height. The pups bumped and tumbled into each other, a cascade of thin legs, black noses, and flying tails, and ricocheted away. Then, with the rhythmic *pflump, pflump, pflump* of their pads striking the gravel, they crossed over to the other side and vanished.

Then it was quiet. My chest rose and fell with a steady tempo. I gazed at the willows that had swallowed the wolves and held on to my last view of them for a long time: haunches lowered as they dug the earth for a burst of speed, the thick hairs on their backs and shoulders rippling like blue-joint grass in a fresh wind.

16

A Face in the Fog

Thirty-six hours ago, to the north of this long barren ridge, I could make out the Stony River, which runs 250 miles from Sled Pass to the Kuskokwim. Now fog blurs the outline of my hunters' tent twenty feet away.

Inside, John and Marshal are quiet, most likely asleep or lost in a book. They are easy to be with, but I am glad for the time to myself. For the third season in a row, I am thinking about not renewing my guide license at the end of the year. The polish has worn off. Herniated disks keep a dull fist pushed into the small of my back. Hours on a cold, wet ridge feel like days. The hunting yarns, the rainsqualls, the smell of sweat, bacon, and over boiled coffee all meld. I suddenly feel filthy. My hair, a mat atop my head, is greasy to the touch. I grab my towel, soap, and shampoo, and step outside.

"You'd better carry a compass, the fog can settle in for days," warned Gary, the outfitter. My neglected old Brunson rides in my pocket. Among the numbers scribbled in the notebook in my left breast pocket is the magnetic bearing from the tents to the nearest pond, less than a quarter-mile away, across a flat of lichen-coated rocks, then down a slight depression. With the bearing dialed in and the needle steady, I follow the arrow into the white. Under my feet is a caribou trail, well worn but shallow in the hard earth. The instrument soon beckons me to angle off to the right, away from the security of the game trail.

Hal Borland wrote that fog is "not quite weather and not altogether mood, yet partaking of both." Yes, it is both, but it is also time. Or rather the slowing down or suspension of time. Mind and body decelerate without protest into a slack water. Legs and arms pendulum and drift, become atmospheric, only partially our own. All vision is peripheral. Through this sea without depth or horizon I move; stones pool like shells about my feet. This damp world is a mirror that reflects back on itself, then back again. Will I step thigh deep into the pond without knowing? Will I veer off my course, swing my feet over the tiny seepage that feeds this basin of water, and walk on into the abyss?

Leaves of brook saxifrage brush the ankles of my hip boots and summon me to stop. The still surface of the pond stretches before me, mist swirling like auroral air above a hot spring on a winter night. But here, I can scarcely tell the difference between air and water temperature as I ease a hand below the liquid surface. A vague outline of grassy hummocks lining the opposite shore fades in and out.

I drape my towel over a stunted willow bush, place the soap and shampoo on a flat stone near the pond's edge and wade in. I close my eyes, splash water on my face, and feel it drip from my nose and chin. It leaves my elbows in droplets, a touch of coolness at each release.

I look up to see bold strokes marking a broad face. Dark lines give way to gray hairs mixed with tinges of red and brown about the muzzle. I do not move. Never before have I seen a wolf materialize from a cloud of vapor. The motionless profile allows me to trace the long guard hairs of massive shoulders down the spine and across the rump before they merge with dark hairs of the crest of the tail.

If all the reasons for me to be here could be distilled and placed into a pair of eyes, it would be the eyes across the pond. The promises that pull me back to guiding are moments like these, when the photographer forgets the camera in his hands or the hunter his rifle. These are the moments when spirit and body meet and become the same. We are two animals alone in the world. Then, in a swirl of cloud, one.

17

Fines and Fine Lines

Hard work yet part vacation, guiding paid my way to many places in Alaska and gave me the opportunity to see a lot of new country. One fall, I was working in the southwest region of the state for an outfitter who seemed to run a respectable operation. Just in from an outer camp, I finished a large meal at the lodge, then wandered down the path for some fresh air.

Even with no one nearby, habit compelled me to step into the thick brush behind the meathouse to relieve myself. While I waited to finish my business, I scanned the area in front of me and noticed something chestnut-brown on the ground. Zipping up, I pushed my way over to find a set of moose antlers. My first thought was that a bear had dragged the antlers away from the meathouse, but didn't get far because of the thicket. Looking closer, I saw that a stout green sapling was set firmly between each antler's widest points. But the sapling was bowed, indicating that it had been forced in place. A cord was tied from the center of the stick to the skull plate and back, then twisted with another stick to apply even more outward pressure.

Someone was trying to stretch a moose rack.

Apparently the antlers didn't spread the fifty inches required to be legal. Had there been four brow tines on just one side, the rack would have been lawful with any size spread, but with only three tines per side, it didn't meet the Alaska Department of Fish and Game sport hunting requirements.

Still, it was a beautiful rack from a mature animal: brown with ivory tips, wide palms, and many points. My best guess was it was extremely close to the fifty-inch minimum, but I left my tape measure in my pocket. I didn't want to confirm what I suspected.

If I knew for sure that the moose was undersized and therefore illegal, I was obligated to report it. Though it was perhaps a loose interpretation of my professional duties, I figured if I didn't measure it, I wouldn't really *know* the antlers were too small.

It was an ingenious idea—I'd never have thought of making a rack for a rack. How much could the antlers be expanded, if at all? An eighth or a quarter of an inch? Maybe that would be enough. Certainly, antlers are more flexible in the summer or early fall when still developing under the nourishing skin called velvet. But it was mid-September. Bulls had already shed their velvet, and the antlers were hard.

I knew a bit about judging trophies in the field, and I understood how difficult it could be. Sometimes obstructions like brush, trees, or grass block the view. Sometimes vision is hampered by wind, rain, or failing light. At two hundred yards, at dusk, when wind shakes your binoculars and rain streaks the lenses, it isn't easy to determine forty-nine and a half inches from fifty inches.

Complicating these problems is the challenge of identifying what qualifies as a point or a tine when regulations make it necessary to count them. (Points are located on the upper part of antlers, tines on the brow, or lower portion.) An antler projection can be considered a point or tine only if it is at least one inch long, and longer than it is wide, with the width measured one inch or more from the tip. That means if you see a projection that is one inch wide at its base and seven-eighths of an inch long—even though it looks like a point and would certainly feel like a point if you were jabbed by it—it is not, technically, a point.

Through the years the folks who write the regulations have improved efforts to communicate restrictions and requirements with explanations, illustrations, and videos. They also offer a bottom-line recommendation: if uncertain, don't shoot. That is sage advice, but occasionally complicated by circumstance.

I recall an experience guiding a deaf client for caribou and moose. His ability to read lips impressed me, but most of our communications were with a notepad and pencil. A blue-collar trophy hunter, he had saved for years to be able to hunt in Alaska. I liked him, but over the course of the hunt, two challenges presented themselves. He was a poor marksman and he was noisy in the woods.

Getting him close to animals was difficult yet necessary. Early on, he managed to take a mature bull caribou. Midway through the week a moose wandered near our chosen lookout spot. With four brow tines on one side, the young bull was legal, but its antlers were unimpressive. We continued to hunt.

When days ran short and we still hadn't been able to get close enough to a larger bull, I questioned the wisdom of passing up that first moose. With little time left, my hopes were raised when I spotted a bull picking his way through the spruce, angling in our general direction. The bull had heavy antlers with broad palms and numerous points. To determine the width I needed to look at him from the front, but he stayed on a course that only gave me a side view. Still, it looked like a decent trophy.

From the side I guessed the antlers were fifty-five inches wide. We couldn't afford to sit and watch—the moose was moving fast. We rumbled our way downhill toward the bull, losing sight of him in the process. Winded, we stopped in a tiny opening that I hoped would put us in the animal's path.

Suddenly, the bull appeared, offering a brief frontal view. My enthusiasm withered. The rack was tall and the outermost points stuck almost straight up. It was not as wide as I had thought—but how much less? The luxury of time didn't exist; I needed to signal the hunter yes or no.

The irony of the situation felt like a flood of regulatory injustice. This moose was physically larger than the first one and its antlers had twice the mass. Likely it was older, and therefore of the age group biologists intended hunters to target. But due to the rules, even though it was a better trophy, its legality was in question. At least in my mind.

That should have been enough for me to shake my head and point my thumb to the ground, but I didn't. Standing beside me was a hunter of modest means with his own particular challenges, who might never have this opportunity again.

Something, maybe a degree of confidence from years of experience, told me it was big enough, that allowing a fudge factor of a few extra inches in width wasn't necessary to give the go ahead. That was a safety net I had always relied on. Yet I had misgivings about making a snap decision when it was literally a matter of inches, or less, and the outcome was irreversible. Following a reluctant nod and the silent mouthing of the word *shoot*, I alone heard the rifle's blasts echo across the valley. Walking up to the lifeless animal and feigning nonchalance, I pulled the tape measure from my pocket and breathed again when the numbers rolled just past fifty-one. I had just squeaked by—enough that no one would question my decision.

But sometimes the line between legal and illegal is even finer.

In the late 1980s my father was hunting the Nelchina River drainage with his brother and nephews. In a brushy area above the river, he spotted a bull that was legal because it had three brow tines on one side, the requirement at the time. He fired and knocked the moose down, but it jumped up and started running. A few shots later, the bull went down for good. When he approached the animal, the first thing he noticed was that something was missing. One of his bullets had taken off an antler—the side that made it legal! The hunting party assembled. After several hours of intensive searching, a nephew found the severed antler.

I don't presume to know my father's thoughts at the time, but if the antler hadn't been found I doubt he would have gone to authorities to explain the situation. He had learned a lesson after his first Alaska sheep hunt back in the early 1960s.

The requirement in those days was that a ram needed a three-quarter or larger curl around the outer surface of the horn. My father shot a ram with a three-quarter curl that he believed was legal. A neighbor urged him to show the animal to officials in charge of a voluntary program set up to gather harvest information.

Two officers examined the ram's horns but they couldn't

agree among themselves if minimum requirements had been met. They confiscated the horns, meat, and hide, and my father's rifle. Over a week later, my father received word that his sheep was in fact determined to be legal. When he picked up his trophy and rifle, the meat was gone. Whether the meat was consumed by someone at the station or allowed to rot, he never found out—but he never forgot the incident.

Such experiences don't necessarily turn honest hunters into bandits, but they tend to discourage people from thinking of the law as an ally. It's a pity there isn't less suspicion on either side of the badge. Years ago, a National Park Ranger stopped by the property where Anne and I now reside year-round. Visits by park personnel are infrequent but usually friendly. I'd never met him before and noticed that his eyes darted around the yard as he talked, as if he was collecting evidence. I don't know what he was hoping to find—maybe a smear of out-of-season moose blood or a snagging hook? Even his questions about the animals I'd seen or what I'd been working on seemed pointed. It felt more like an investigation than a visit. I was relieved when he left.

The job of protecting fish and game resources is important, but I wish it were possible to enforce rules with a more liberal application of common sense. Sometimes enforcement is too steadfast in its desire to conform to the letter of the law. Folks who have tried to follow the rules and misjudged, or not understood a confusing regulation deserve leniency. Other times, enforcement officers try to thwart serious violators, but the court system is an impediment to their efforts, and bandits get away with crimes or are allowed to operate for too long. These are the folks who truly deserve scrutiny.

While guiding for brown bear on the Alaska Peninsula near the mouth of the Beaver River in the spring of 1982, I noticed a Super Cub circling repeatedly in an area about three miles upriver. The distance was too far for me to read the airplane's identification numbers, but I noted its red color. Several days later, as I was leading clients in the same location, we climbed a ridge to glass the valley below. It didn't take long to spot a dead caribou lying in the middle of an open field. We made our way to the caribou and found one bullet hole in the chest. The animal was otherwise untouched.

We assumed a bandit had shot the caribou, with plans to return later in the hopes that a trophy bear had been drawn to his "bait station." That afternoon we watched a sow and two cubs discover, then begin to feast on the caribou. We reported the incident to authorities on our return to camp. When an officer investigated three days later, he admitted he knew who it was, but for now he was keeping an eye on him in an effort to get rock-solid evidence that would hold up in court.

Though the burden of proof can protect the innocent, it is also often a reason outlaws aren't convicted of their crimes—or at least not all of them. A neighbor told me about one such incident that happened near his Lake Clark lodge.

On an early morning flightseeing trip up the Chulitna River with two friends, Chuck spotted a large bull moose. After a good look from the air at the bull and a nearby cow, they returned to the lodge for the day.

That afternoon, Chuck heard a Cessna 206 fly upriver.

Shortly after, a Super Cub departed from the same area. It didn't take Chuck long to put two and two together. A local outfitter habitually left his Super Cub, on wheels, parked on a sandbar of the Chulitna. His 206, on floats, was normally kept at a protected bay on the other side of Lake Clark.

Chuck was convinced that the outfitter was using his floatplane to locate moose, then landing in the river where the Cub was parked. An assistant guide and hunter would be shuttled in the Cub—a smaller, more maneuverable airplane—to a location near the moose.

At day's end Chuck flew back to the area. There were two people packing meat from the dead bull up the hill toward a ridge where it looked like a Cub could land. His suspicions were confirmed.

Since the bull had been alive in the morning and it was illegal to fly then hunt the same day, Chuck called in the authorities. It went to trial. On the witness stand Chuck admitted he hadn't seen the airplanes come and go, but by their sound he could tell one was a Cub and the other a Cessna on floats. The jury didn't believe anyone could tell the difference in airplanes by their sound from a mile away. Neither the outfitter, his crew, or the hunter was convicted of same-day airborne hunting, though an assistant guide was cited for not having a guide license.

The outfitter held a grudge. Every time he flew by Chuck's place he would buzz low over the lodge roof. One day, fed up, Chuck went outside with his shotgun when he heard the airplane approaching. When the plane was directly over the lodge Chuck swung the shotgun and faked a recoil by jerking his shoulder back. The pilot and passengers couldn't hear that the shotgun hadn't gone off, but it must have *looked* like he had fired. Chuck could see their eyes were wide as they streaked by. They never came back.

Sometimes the guilty get their due. Ron Hayes was perhaps the most infamous of all Alaska guides. I recall meeting him when I was a neophyte guide and he was a star of the profession. He was fit and had the rugged looks and posture of a confident outdoorsman. He attracted high rollers and hangers-on. His popularity was based on his success rate—his clients got bears—big ones—with amazing regularity.

As a pilot, Hayes was skilled at spotting grizzlies from the air, then driving them with his airplane to a hunter waiting on the ground. In the early 1980s he was caught doing just that. He lost his guide license and a couple of aircraft and received a fine.

Soon afterward he began operating a sport fishing lodge in southwest Alaska. His new endeavor attracted wealthy clients, some who wanted to hunt. Unable to resist, Hayes offered his expertise in such matters to handpicked clients, though he tried to keep his underhand airborne operation a secret.

In time Hayes was again caught using his airplane to drive a bear toward a waiting client. He paid a six-figure fine, lost five more airplanes, and served time in jail. For a documentary on poaching, Hayes re-created his method of using a plane to frighten bears in the direction of a hunter. In the film Hayes admitted that he helped over three dozen of his clients place grizzlies in the Boone and Crockett Club's record book using the same illegal technique.

Another outfitter who was a flagrant violator not only of game laws, but of laws in general, was John Graybill.

Graybill had a history of fish and game violations in Michigan before he was first convicted in Alaska in 1971 for illegal use of an aircraft. He was forced to forfeit his airplane to the state. Following that conviction was another for illegal possession of a brown bear hide and subsequent probation violations.

In 1980 news spread in sketchy details through guiding circles about Graybill's latest stunt. He had been caught poaching moose in Katmai National Park and set his own airplane on fire to keep it from being seized. The story I got was that Graybill saw agents emerge out of the bushes and knew he'd been caught red-handed. On impulse, he grabbed a can of gas, splashed it on his airplane, and torched it. The actual event may have played out slightly differently, but the result of the tale was that Graybill, at least for a time, achieved folk hero status, like an Alaska guide version of Jesse James.

It wasn't the poaching part of the story, but the defiant spontaneity and the pure imagination of his pyromaniacal exploit that caused even the most law-abiding folks to shake their heads with something akin to admiration. But not for long.

Graybill's criminal episodes continued. He was convicted of twenty fish and game violations, which included same-day airborne hunting, the use of an airplane to herd brown bear, hunting without a license, and use of explosives to drive a bear to a hunter. An investigation followed for the illegal killing of wolves in Denali National Park and a series of related theft, trespass, and burglary activities occurring outside of park boundaries. As the judge told him, "I think that at some point you've got to learn that the State of Alaska is not your private hunting reserve, Mr. Graybill. . . ."

He finally went to prison for a lengthy stay.

The history of violations and injustices pertaining to fish and game resources in Alaska offers a rich sampler of cases on both sides of the issue. When I look from one viewpoint at the challenges of enforcement, I see that too much rigidity risks losing supporters. Yet at the same time it seems in many cases that laws aren't strict enough. I become angry and indignant, and hope the books thrown at the perpetrators are heavy hardbound tomes, hurled with great accuracy.

What is fair and what is not gets even more complicated for some of us who believe commercial users of resources should be held to higher standards. Although I don't endorse taking a moose, caribou, or trout out-of-season just because one wants to eat it, there is a huge difference between subsistence violations and the conduct of people like Hayes and Graybill.

As each new season arrives, I do my best to read the regulations and follow them. But I have as much potential for error as anyone.

Several years ago in the middle of the winter, I drilled a couple of holes in the ice to make two sets (setlines) for burbot, an ugly but tasty freshwater relative of the lingcod. Fresh meat of any kind is a rarity during the cold months for Anne and me, and except for an occasional grouse, we'd been eating from the fish and meat we'd jarred during the summer and fall. I caught one burbot and Anne fried it for dinner. After eating, I looked at the calendar and suddenly realized that a new year had arrived and my fishing license had expired. For the past week the weather had kept me from making a trip across the lake to get our mail and purchase a new license. There was no intent to do wrong. I'd simply forgotten.

I felt a pang of guilt for not being able to live up to my own standards, but it quickly faded. Those sweet, firm fillets lightly floured and fried in olive oil until golden-brown had sure tasted good.

Three

Settled In

Getting There

18

VGRTNLL. My letters are as dismal as the weather, and the grid of words on the board in front of me contains no open vowels. The outcome of this Scrabble game is the only thing I can predict. Anne will win, as she has for almost a year straight. Through the one window we haven't boarded up yet I peer at low clouds.

It is a still, drizzly morning. A two hundred-foot ceiling lies above the surface of the water. Here, at its upper end, Lake Clark is four miles wide, though the visibility is down to half that distance. I can barely make out the islands in front of our place.

Low-pressure systems are common in the month of August. They work their way up the Aleutians, moving like blimps toward the Gulf of Alaska, sometimes stalling out around Kodiak or Bristol Bay, sometimes making their way aimlessly into Canada. I have no way of knowing how long we will have to postpone our two-and-a-half-hour flight back to town.

With no phone or television, our only option for getting a weather report is for me to taxi our Super Cub half a mile out into the lake, where I can make a line-of-sight radio connection with the relay station. But the airplane sits on a trailer on the rocky beach. Because there is no protected cove here, we must use a manual winch to pull it to dry ground after every flight. I consider the effort involved in confirming what I already suspect—*VFR Not Recommended*—and decide to wait.

"When do you think it will clear up?" Anne asks as she lays *rotgut* down on a triple word. Even winning, she is anxious to go. We have let the fire die out, and she is wearing gloves and a fleece jacket. "I'll walk down to the beach and check," I offer.

To the west the overcast is brighter. This is how it normally clears out, from the direction of Bristol Bay. I judge it will be at least two hours before I'll consider taking off. The Cub is ready to go, crammed full of things we need to take back to town—mostly garbage. Anne and our dog Cassie will take up the remaining space.

Three hours pass before the clouds lift enough to reveal the couloir on Copper Mountain that marks the fifteen hundred-foot level. We push our chairs away from the table when we hear the eastbound rumble of a de Havilland Beaver on floats. We stand up and start for the door when, moments later, a Cessna 185 follows it into Lake Clark Pass.

Forty minutes later, we are airborne near the mouth of the Tlikakila River. We follow its turbid flow past Otter Lake, Moose Pasture, and Glacier Fork. It takes most of an hour to get beyond Summit Lake to the southeast bend in the pass that is the start of what we locals refer to as The Narrows. This is a common weather bottleneck. The ceiling has come down, but the visibility is still five miles.

We enter the aptly named passage, hugging the steep slope of the mountain on our right. The accepted traffic pattern used to separate east and westbound aircraft gives maximum room to execute an about face if needed. I pull back on the throttle and trim to half flaps, reducing my airspeed. The mountain passes by my wing tip a little more slowly. It is gray up ahead. In minutes, my level of concern has gone from moderate to high. But we have time and gas invested, and before I turn around I want to see if things improve on the other side. Anne's brother, who lives half the year on Cook Inlet's coast, has a term for weather like this. I can't remember if it's *scuddy* or *skunky*. I think it looks *crappy*, and decide to wait it out at nearby Big River Lakes. We have never had to land here before. I ease the airplane through the increasing murk and touch down on the surface of the northernmost lake.

Drizzle thickens on the windshield, forms beads, and runs down in droplets. I slide back the scratched portside window and lean my head out. A gunmetal gray greets my eyes. Along the serpentine shoreline of marsh there is no solid place to get out and stretch our legs. We are safe, yet the fist of my right hand holds the control stick tightly in my lap. My left hand cups the throttle. Our spirits are as damp as this border of wetland and water. I turn for a distant shore where land rises steeply to form a ridge. Anne hands me half a salmon sandwich. "Thanks," I say, then swing my microphone from my lips. I chew to the steady *thump, thump, thump* of the engine.

Behind Anne, under our dog, a box of used books sits on bags of washed plastic containers and smashed cans. Beneath the trash is survival gear: a revolver, a tarp, mosquito headnets, freeze-dried stew, and stale candy bars. I imagine our camp if we are forced to spend the night: a tarp hung between alders, water dripping from its edges, the down in our sleeping bags clumping as we lie on a cross-hatch of branches in an attempt to keep us off the soggy earth. I can smell our hair, pungent with smoke after our feeble efforts to kindle a fire with small sticks of wet willow.

Following the promise of drier ground, we taxi toward the far shore and locate the only clearing wide enough in the dense brush to accommodate the thirty-six-foot wingspan of our airplane. Two straw-colored hummocks lie near the water's edge. I begin to shut the engine down when one of the hummocks moves, then the other. We watch the brown bear and her two-year-old cub mill around, upturned noses twitching in our direction. As the last of my sandwich slides down my throat, I step hard on the right rudder.

"Not to complain or anything, but my butt's sore and Cassie has bad breath," Anne grumbles.

"Let's look over in that bight." I nod my head to the north. Through the sinking stratus cloud that caps the lake, the landing light of an airplane appears. Then a Beaver on floats slowly carves out a silhouette above the water and touches down. "Looks like someone else decided to wait out the weather," I say. We watch as the pilot pulls up to a tiny grassy island, unloads four people, hops back in and takes off, disappearing into the soup.

I hold no kind thoughts for the air-taxi pilot who appears so skillful and brave. I have no intention of taking off in this weather. It is the slate-colored flat light that concerns me most.

Years ago I departed Farewell Lake under innocuous skies, bound for Big Lake, fifty-two miles north of Anchorage. It was early spring and the ground was covered with a fresh layer of snow. Halfway there, near Widgeon Lake, the ceiling started settling and the ridges took on a fuzzy look. Seasoned pilots had taught me that the most likely impasse was still miles ahead; I descended to a lower altitude, following occasional patches of willow that loosely sketched out the shape of Ptarmigan Valley. By degrees, the clouds above and the snow below crept toward a sameness of tone.

A dark streak of brush suddenly flashed just over my right wing tip. In a panic, I made a steep 180-degree turn and headed back toward the dim entrance of Rainy Pass. What I had mistaken for clouds on my right had been a solid, rocky mountain that extended from the main range out into the valley floor. All the way back to Farewell Lake I kept thinking of the phrase: "Better three days late than thirty years too soon."

Those words come back to me now as I edge the plane near shore. Another brown bear steps out to greet us. Our floats cut shallow V's through the water as we idle once again toward the center of the lake.

"When do you think we can go?" Anne asks.

"I don't know," I reply.

I pull the mixture control and watch the prop slow to a stop. The silence, at least, is welcome. I remove my headset and turn the key to the off position. "We'll just have to wait."

As we float there, I think about how big Alaska really is—how when the weather knuckles down on you, the feeling of remoteness intensifies, but the vastness is gone. Maybe a desire to reclaim that sense of openness urges one to push on, or perhaps it is simply the lure of comfort waiting on the other end that keeps us going. Most of us who pilot boats or airplanes have, more than once, turned a defiant but foolish face against the elements to reach some destination.

Here I am, sitting in a cramped cockpit with no good place

to park, anxious about the weather, and wanting to get the hell where I'm going. It all feels too familiar, and makes me think about other times I faced similar decisions on whether to keep traveling.

The murky air, the mist and clouds around us, remind me of an experience I had years ago when the foggy weather I tried to force my way through was entirely in my head. The vehicle I was operating was neither airplane nor boat.

It was a Coot—a jeep-like, articulated four-wheel drive with no cab. Stan Frost asked me to drive it from one mountain camp to another. Just after breakfast Stan flew me, a sack lunch, and a spare engine to the lower camp. We removed the old engine, installed the spare, and made sure it started. Stan took off. He would give me all day to get the Coot to the upper camp, then land there that evening to pick me up.

This was going to be an easy trip, I thought. It was only four miles up a wide open river valley with no deep water to cross. Even at a slow speed I should arrive in less than an hour and a half.

The charms of a Coot are few—basically it is a steel mule, an alternative to packing loads on your back. The engine is noisy, the steering is stiff, and the suspension has all the shock absorption qualities of a stump.

I bounced and rattled my way along a short trail, then rolled down a steep gravel bank to the main riverbed. I turned southeast, felt the wind on the back of my head, and smelled exhaust wafting over my shoulders. The breeze wasn't strong, but it flowed up the valley at about the same speed I was driving, its angle perfect to funnel fumes directly to my seat. As I gazed through clear air at mountain vistas and scanned the hillsides for game, it seemed strange to be inhaling the noxious odor of a city street. I sped up, trying to outrun the stink, but the engine kicked out even more fumes and the vapor wrapped around me like a nasty shawl. I backed off on the throttle, then stood up to steer, but that didn't get my head above the fumes.

Then, with less than a mile behind me, the engine began clinking and clanking. Shortly after, the Coot stopped moving. I shut it off, moved the bench seat to the side, and peered into the engine compartment. I didn't know much about engines beyond the basics: sparkplugs need to spark, carburetors need gas and air, and if something is loose, tighten it. Amid the oil and grime, I noticed some loose bolts, but the space was so cramped I couldn't get a wrench on the bolt heads.

The reprieve was welcome, but my head ached as I stared at my unexpected problem. I dug out the tool kit. It didn't contain much beyond adjustable wrenches, a pair of pliers, screwdrivers, and bailing wire. The better part of an hour passed while I fiddled with disconnecting, removing, tightening, then re-installing the engine. It ran.

As soon as I was driving again, the fumes returned with a vengeance. I decided to treat the smell as a nuisance or irritant—like hiking with a sore toe or working amid swarms of mosquitoes. After all, I was driving a vehicle with no top up a valley in the middle of the Alaska Range, and I knew that the exhaust gas most to be feared was odorless.

My stomach began doing gymnastics—nothing much, just a lazy somersault south of the belly button. I thought the churning might be my body's call for food. Shutting the engine off, I dug out my lunch, took a half-hearted bite from a sandwich, and almost spat it out. I managed to choke down half of it, but it didn't settle my stomach.

Ideas of an enjoyable trip vanished. I merely wanted to get to my destination and turn the machine off for good. I tied a bandana across my face, started the Coot, and aimed up-river. I scanned the smoothest route through the gravel immediately in front of me, then my mind and steering wandered simultaneously. When the tires bumped into some large stones, I caught myself and turned the wheel back to center. It became a pattern: scan, drift, veer, steer—again and again. All the while, my eyeballs ached, as if my head was in a clamp. Then, once again, the Coot stopped moving.

I sat there staring for some time before it occurred to me to turn the key to the off position. Removing an engine a second time is supposed to be faster than the first, but it wasn't working out that way. I fixed my gaze on the choke and throttle cables, and thought, *oh, those need to be disconnected*. Then I picked up a wrench and turned it over in my hand, marveling at its heft and the pattern of rust on its side.

It was like having dreams of being a mechanic, broken with interludes of slow-witted awe. I'd glance at my watch to see how much of the day was slipping by, but I couldn't recall where the hands were the last time I looked. In the middle of the foggy dream, the engine rumbled back to life, its sound flooding me with both dread and relief.

I felt as single-minded as a man with scattered thoughts could.

Gotta get there.

Don't let Stan down.

Job to do.

My focus narrowed to a clump of willows ahead—from

that point I should be able to see the camp. I rattled my way upriver.

He'll understand.

Just turn it off and walk.

The urge to *get there*, my ill-conceived imperative to continue, was losing momentum. Finally, I pulled even with the willow bushes and saw the wall tent. I turned off the machine. A break is what I need, I thought. I'll walk to the tent and lie down—then finish the job later.

Even walking, I couldn't maintain a straight line or hold my thoughts for long. My head buzzed and my stomach churned on my clumsy zigzag to the tent. I lay down on a cot and watched the canvas ceiling spin while I waited for Stan. I had never fully appreciated the dangers of carbon monoxide poisoning.

On the Cub ride back to the lodge I was able to keep the contents of my stomach where they belonged, but walking the short distance down from the strip I retched four times. Later, sitting in the lodge, with my head in my hands, feeling like hell, I couldn't appreciate my good fortune: On a whim, Stan had recently purchased oxygen to bolster his first aid supplies. And oxygen was what the doctor who Stan made radio contact with recommended: ten minutes every hour, until the following morning. "Keep an eye on him," the doctor said. That wouldn't be difficult. It took days to clear my foggy brain, ease my headache's viselike grip, and regain an appetite.

Had the insidious vapors not muddled my judgment, perhaps I'd have walked away from the Coot earlier. I like to think so, but I was in the grip not only of the fumes but of my drive to reach a goal—a trait I share with plenty of others, particularly other Alaskan men. Informing that urge is the knowledge that if you can't do a job, there are plenty of other men who can. Maybe *getting there* is a yardstick held up to judge peers, mentors, ourselves.

Stopping at Big River Lakes to wait out the weather was one time I showed good judgment. The rest of that trip was uneventful. After a two-hour wait, the weather cleared enough for us to reach our destination. Unfortunately, my track record since then is hardly unblemished. On two flights, Anne offered a voice of reason from the back seat of the Cub: "Do you think this is a good idea?" as I entered The Narrows in Lake Clark Pass on a particularly congested August morning, and "What about returning to Long Lake?" when we followed the Glenn Highway from Eureka to Palmer, trying to outrace an approaching storm. I was flying IFR—I Follow Road, or I Follow River pilots like to joke—but it's only funny when you have arrived safely.

On the other hand, the resolve to travel only in perfect weather would result in few trips. And if I'd never tiptoed to the edge of my comfort level, I'd have lost opportunities to improve my skills.

Neither is Anne immune from the desire to get there, especially when it involves retrieving her mail. The winter of 2000–2001 produced a series of storms, one after the next, that kept Lake Clark ice free and its waters churned to a froth. We hadn't been able to get to the post office, located on the opposite shore of the lake, for over two weeks. Anne's anxiousness and irritation grew. She glared at the lake's rough surface as if the water itself was plotting against her. "Maybe it's not as bad as it looks," she suggested. Several times, she talked about making the twenty-six mile round-trip run in our open skiff.

Against my better judgment, I gave in one morning when the winds eased up to reveal, not a calm surface, but fewer whitecaps. More than the slightly encouraging trend in the weather, what changed my mind was Anne's declaration, "If you don't want to go, I'll go myself."

It was warm for mid-January in Alaska, but still only a few degrees above freezing. Anne sat on loose float cushions in the bow, wearing a bright orange exposure suit. As soon as we were out of our bay, we were running with the waves. The ride was bumpier than expected, but after a few minutes, I eased into the lake's rhythm.

Distracted by the motion of swells and the effort of steering, I barely noticed the deepening troughs, the breaking crests. Anne's posture stiffened and she shot nervous glances past the stern and over both gunwales. I glimpsed behind me and thought, *holy crap, this is big water!* We were in the middle of the lake, over one of its deepest parts—more than eight hundred feet—alone. Our eighteen-foot boat felt like it was shrinking beneath us. We were probably the only people on the entire lake still using a boat so late in the season. If we got into trouble, there wouldn't be any help coming. No one would even know to search for us until they noticed our skiff missing or found the note I left on our kitchen counter: BOATED TO PORT ALSWORTH, 1-18, NOON.

Turning around halfway would mean no mail, a long and wet ride home, and a dicey 180-degree maneuver in big waves. I thought about it for a few minutes, then shouted above the outboard's din that we should head home. Anne nodded in agreement.

I rode up and over several big waves, searching ahead for a slight lessening of wave height or a lengthening of the distance between crests. An opportunity approached and I counted down its arrival like a blast off: *Three, two, one.* Twisting the throttle to full just as the skiff topped a wave, I angled down, then turned the boat sideways, completing a hasty but controlled U-turn. The vibration of the tiller handle in my gloved palm was a reminder that although the outboard was running we would be swamped in an instant if it quit. With the bow pointed back into the waves I was forced to adjust the throttle constantly to keep the waves from breaking into the open boat.

When we finally pulled into the protection of our bay, getting back felt every bit as good as getting there, but I refrained from self-congratulation. Turning around wasn't much to brag about, especially when good judgment followed too slowly on the heels of a poor decision. What in hair-raising hell were we thinking, ever starting out in the first place? Of course, we assured ourselves, we would never attempt such a trip again. We'd learned our lesson. This time.

19

Return

On the north shore of Lake Clark where Anne and I now live, an old cache stands between our cabin and the beach. A few summers ago, I discovered rot in each of the four legs when the blade of my pocketknife slid easily to its hilt. These uprights have already been replaced once, but twenty years is pretty much what you get when a spruce log is used as a foundation post. Diagonal log braces lag-bolted to the legs serve as a provisional repair. It would surely be improper to offer this building chemically treated posts, cut and shipped from thousands of miles away, as its only physical connection with the land. Something will eventually have to be done, but for now the new log supports are sound and pleasing to the eye, and graciously offer a bit more time.

Just east of our place is Brown's cabin. Brown Carlson was a fisherman and trapper, and the first permanent Euro-American settler on Lake Clark. After his death in 1975, his daughter, Ida, tried to stave off deterioration of his home during her sporadic and brief visits to the property.

After a decade or so she stopped coming, and for years the building sat untouched. Now the three-sided logs of his cabin chevron down against each side of a vertical, full-dimension, rough-cut two-by-eight. That lone spruce board neatly divides the cabin's thirty-foot length in half. On each side of the upright, from eave to moist earth, empty space forms a pattern of v's where the logs have separated, revealing the lower two of three nails that hold each log in place.

The sagging roofline follows the suggestion down. On the north side, where a lean-to addition held moisture against the building for years, the logs are rotten seven rounds high. The bottom of the wall has shifted a foot inward from its middle foundation post.

The heavy plank floor rises here and dips there, not unlike the surface of the lake during a southeast blow. A white enamel wood-burning cook stove rests in the middle of the cabin, away from a hole in the roof where the stove pipe once stood. When rain enters it forms dark puddles below the opening. The ceiling boards are a deep auburn from wood and pipe smoke, and, like almost everything else, lowest in the middle. The door no longer fits its jamb and must be tied to keep it shut.

Follow the shore eastbound, up the bear trail where it leads over a steep ridge to Onion Bay, past three rocky fingers to the outside beach, continue until the angular rocks underfoot turn to gravel. There, on a twisted piece of driftwood nailed to an aspen, hang loose coils of a decayed manila rope. Behind the protection of a small stand of white spruce, a rusty pitcher pump protrudes from the ground. Beyond the pump sits another abandoned cabin.

The five-gallon gas cans that Joe Thompson, a local prospector and contemporary of Brown's, flattened and squared to cover his roof are badly rusted, yet still shed the rain. His cabin is less than half the size of Brown's, but if you look past the mess bears have made, more structurally intact. Still, the bedroom addition is listing, sinking into the ground. His woodshed collapsed years ago and the cache legs are porcupine-gnawed and soft where they disappear into the earth.

Spread throughout Alaska are cabins in various stages of breakdown, some with names like Brown and Joe still attached to them, others fading into the earth a step behind our memory of their human inhabitants. I have been fortunate to observe many such dwellings, a few no more than rectangular hedges of spruce and paper birch growing from the remains of log walls. Lately, when I stand at one of these sites, I am less concerned with permanence than I once was. I loved to look through log cabin books, at photos of huge knee braces supporting a hand-hewn beam, telltale broadaxe marks along its sides. Maybe I felt strength in buildings would reflect brawn and vitality in me. Now as I slide beyond the middle stage of my own life, my views are changing. I still understand the wisdom in building homes and boats to weather storms, but I have a new appreciation—not for shoddy craftsmanship that might lead to collapse, but for the transient nature of things. I think about the conservationist practice of leaving no trace in the wilderness, and how easily we humans separate ourselves from that ethic when we return to an enduring world of steel, cement, and plastic.

There is something in most of us that seeks a lasting mark of our existence. Maybe one reason for writing down my adventures is to leave a permanent record. Certainly there is an element of ego at work in the desire to publish stories based on my own life. Could I ever follow the example of Li Po, the Chinese poet, who amused himself by casting his crafted lines into a stream to watch them sail away?

Twenty years ago I frequented an old Iditarod roadhouse that lies roughly 130 miles away from my present home, its leaning moss-covered walls settling more each year into the valley floor. Though this cool northern climate is slow to re-claim log cabins and to heal scars on the land, someday some-one will walk across the collapsed sod roof of that cabin on Dalzell Creek and never guess what lies beneath his or her feet. I wonder if there could be a better legacy than building a cabin that will eventually become part of the earth.

20

The Wake

If an ass goes traveling, he'll not come back a horse.
—THOMAS FULLER, MD

John had dashed off a quick note that he wanted to go "LITE"—
no stove, no food we had to cook or heat—not even the freeze-
dried variety. Regarded as an authority on the history of
the Lake Clark and Iliamna Lake region, John was revered,
and sometimes feared, for his hiking prowess. It was with
a bit of trepidation that I had accepted his offer to join him
on a sheep hunt.

Though I hadn't been training to climb mountains, the
cabin Anne and I built sits on a hill, and I make many trips
a day up and down the inclined path. I was in tip-top shape—
for climbing one hundred yards. I was hoping my experience guiding sheep hunters almost a decade before would
retroactively boost me to the top of the mountain.

The first day of the hunt was forecast to be clear, but when
I woke a blanket of fog lay over the surface of the lake. The
plan was for me to drive my skiff fourteen miles across the
lake to Port Alsworth to meet John, then depart on foot for
alpine country.

From the shore, under the bank of clouds, I could make
out the three small islands one and a half miles distant.
Beyond that, fog whitened out the lake and sky. Still, visibility as far as the islands was a good sign. Surely the fog
would burn off rapidly, I thought, maybe even by the time

I finished my coffee and oatmeal. I kissed Anne and she wished me a sleepy, "Good luck." I jumped in the boat and pulled out of our bay.

Just past the last island to the south loomed a wall of white. I slowed, wondering why I hadn't packed my compass. But the obstacle seemed easy enough. Lake Clark is long and narrow, only about four miles wide. By cutting straight across to the south side, I figured I could follow the shoreline to my destination. I had extra gas and plenty of time, and the hope that any moment the bow of my skiff would break into sunshine. Since I couldn't see much in front of me, I decided to set a course by watching the boat's wake. That technique had more or less worked for me and a couple of buddies years ago. Caught in fog on the south side of Kachemak Bay, we reached the north side safely, although we ended up missing our mark by a mile. What I didn't realize was that it was the incoming waves caused by a light breeze, more than our wake, that helped steer our course.

I locked my left arm and started out, but the track my boat cut through the water formed a slight curve. No problem: I pulled the tiller toward me to compensate, arrow straight and dead on. The satisfaction was short-lived. Glancing back in the ensuing moments, I again noticed that unmistakable curve. I thought about advice that I'd received from a pilot friend about maintaining a course. Sometimes, he said, when you are flying, don't adjust the rudder left or right, just *think* about making those adjustments. So I thought. But those synaptic suggestions didn't pass as successfully down the length of my arm as they did from my friend's head to his feet. The fog thickened and my confidence thinned while I constantly adjusted direction.

Soon I realized it was taking me far too long to reach the shore. I peered anxiously over the bow hoping I could make out a familiar landmark. Before long, I saw the sketchy outline of a group of scraggly spruce projecting from a stony bluff. As I inched ahead, I saw that it wasn't the shore after all, but an island. *There are no islands on this side of the lake*, I thought, bewildered. The boat drew a little closer and I recognized it then as the islet located between Miller Creek and Priest Rock that lies four miles west of our cabin, on the north side of the lake. Somehow, I had managed a giant U-turn. With the knowledge that I tended to steer too much to the right of center, I again pointed the bow toward the south shore and headed back into the fog, adjusting my course a little to the left.

I knew that if I angled too far to the right again, I could end up running down the middle of the lake, using up gas and time without making land. Correcting a bit too far left could only deliver me farther east, but at least I would be on the south shore.

In fog, time slows to an absurd creep. I couldn't pull the contour of terra firma out of the murk in front of me. There was neither wind nor heat enough from the sun to break the grip of clouds clinging to the surface of earth and water. The skiff crawled on as if surrounded by curtains of felt, with the only sense of motion the brief slip and swirl of water against the gunwales. Then an outline of trees appeared. To my amazement and chagrin, this time it was not an island, but *two* islands. I looked beyond them to an odd shape near the shore: an airplane. Then I registered its color. Yellow. It was *my* airplane! I'd made a counter-clockwise loop and ended up almost back home.

I glanced at my watch and realized I was slipping behind schedule. With no time now to even feel embarrassment, I twisted the outboard's throttle wide open and raced to our dock. My old compass would be the ticket, but I couldn't recall where I'd stored it. I'd just grab my GPS from the airplane and try again.

Not wanting to worry my wife, I sprinted up the hill to explain my return. She was still asleep when I burst through the door. Winded from my dash, I condensed the explanation of my reappearance into one utterance. "Heybabe—*Wheeez*—everything'sfine gotturnedaroundinthefog—*Wphuue*—I'm gonnatryagain—*Wheeez*—loveyabye." I ran down the trail, snatched my GPS, jumped in the boat, and took off.

I flipped up the antenna and turned on the handheld unit. It always takes a few minutes to gather enough satellite signals to make a triangulation before the instrument provides a bearing. A bold bar appears on a graph for each connection made to a satellite. *Acquiring*, the screen reads, as the bars emerge one at a time, eventually forming a cityscape of blocky towers. Believing that a heading would appear any second, I drove on until I plunged again into the wall of white.

Besides the location of my compass, there was something else I'd forgotten: The GPS rollover day had just occurred. The rollover happens approximately once every twenty years, when the system resets itself. Reportedly, data during this time can be processed and displayed incorrectly, and some older receivers can fail for up to a week. Those facts, unfortunately, had been stored away in the foggier recesses of my gray matter.

I put the steering-by-wake method behind me. Speeding

along, I peered intently over the bow for a sign of land, ready to cut the throttle in an instant. The fog washed around me and the screen on the GPS hung in electronic limbo. *Acquiring, Acquiring, Acquiring . . .* Then miraculously, the GPS made it through the doldrums. I slowed down and punched in Tommy Island, which sits just outside of Hardenburg Bay, where I was to meet John. The fog spirits must have been tired of laughing at me, or decided to take pity, because somehow my course was accurate. The GPS indicated that Tommy Island was just three miles away. Anxiety drained out of me and I relaxed. I even started to feel a bit cocky. What's the big deal, it's an easy ride from here, I thought. Then the screen suddenly went blank and the words *Poor GPS Coverage* appeared.

Over the next few miles, the GPS yo-yoed between being a direction finder and a worthless piece of plastic. About the time I was beginning to doubt its existence, Tommy Island emerged through the clouds. I angled left and intercepted the shoreline, using its rocky contour as a guide. Just before reaching the entrance to the bay, I broke out of the fog.

In the distance, the beach was awash in brilliant sun as if it had been that way for hours. At the water's edge, John paced back and forth pounding the gravel to submission with his boots. I looked at my watch, surprised to find I was only fifteen minutes late.

Anxious to be underway, John offered to drop off my outbound mail at the nearby post office while I tied up my boat and changed gear. I discarded my warm float coat in favor of a lightweight jacket, peeled off my hip boots, and laced up my climbing boots. When John returned, he told me that Eric, a friend of his, was joining us.

After brief introductions, John suggested that we each carry part of the tent I had brought along. I divided it up, and with some misguided machismo, kept the heaviest portion for myself. It was then that I got my first look at the differences in our packs. Mine was an external frame with a sturdy, multi-pocketed nylon bag. It held, among other things, a sleeping bag and pad, a water bottle, extra socks, and two knives. *My* idea of going "LITE" was leaving my camera at home and paring down my first aid kit. Eric's pack was a newer, internal frame model of similar proportions and load to mine. John's pack was, by comparison, anorexic: lashed on a bare-bones aluminum frame was a cloth bag. I wondered if it was large enough to contain even a small sleeping bag. When I asked about water bottles, Eric said he had two. John reached in his pocket and produced a quart-sized Ziploc, explaining that was all he needed if he had to carry water.

Following a trail several miles through a boreal forest brought us to Kontrashibuna Lake. There, under the branches of a large spruce, we located the old canoe that John had permission to use. After a hasty loading, I grabbed a paddle and crawled over our gear to the bow. Across the lake and up the far shore we moved steadily, until John steered us onto a tiny gravel beach. I craned my neck to look up at a mountain that rose steeply from turquoise water to a cornflower-blue sky.

John didn't sprint, but he didn't stop either. Eric was fit from recent trips in the mountains and climbed easily. My breathing soon became labored. I wondered if a race had started and no one had issued me a bib number. It was quickly apparent that I needed a way to slow John down. Someone had told me that there was only one way to get John to stop for any length of time: discuss history. He loved to talk about the region's rich past. I plumbed the recesses of my brain for a fitting topic. "Did the Capps Expedition bring horses into this area?" I asked. I was too busy sucking in air and plotting my next question to listen to his unwinded and all too succinct reply.

A couple of inclines later I stammered, "How big was the mining operation at Kasna Creek?" That bought a little more time, but not enough oxygen, because I was still puffing when he finished answering and resumed the climb. I should have prepared more inquiries, as I was already using up my shallow reserve of local knowledge. Worse yet, John was catching on to my sudden interest in regional lore. After that, he didn't let me get close enough to even pose a question.

When John and Eric stopped to glass a band of sheep, I finally caught up. If this had been an Olympic event, I had a stranglehold on the bronze. I flopped down beside them just as they rose to continue upward. Behind us, the northeast side of the sloped mountain we were ascending plunged recklessly in jutting fingers of solid rock and loose rubble. To look down its steep face was an invitation to vertigo, while the weather-hardened surface to the southwest held grasses and lichens in gently inclining, undulating folds. From near the summit I could see the mountain's shoulder drop off quickly, hiding a valley below. In that saddle, John said, was a prime place to camp, near a lake.

I tried to suppress the joy I felt when we reached the water. The muscles of my legs were rubbery with a sensation that seemed to vibrate through every bone. Just the idea of a full night's rest jump-started my depleted reserves. I unlaced my boots and pulled off my socks to let my toes wiggle in the alpine air. Mountain water slid easily down my throat and I munched on handfuls of trail mix. I leaned my head back and shut my eyes. Then I heard John say it was too early in the day to stop. It was like meandering in the fog that morning, when I believed my destination near at hand, only to discover I had to begin again. Although I understood the wisdom of climbing to the next bench in theoretical terms, I dreaded pressing on.

When I reached the top of the bench, John and Eric stood next to their packs. The ground was boulder-strewn but flat. A seepage gurgled nearby. Ah, I thought, a place to camp at last; somehow I'd made it. Already I envisioned settling my backside into a sleeping pad-cushioned contour of alpine terrain, the perfect fit of hump to hip, dip to derrière. John interrupted my reverie. "There is plenty of daylight left, we should leave our packs here, climb up and walk the ridge before calling it a night." I eyed the slope and thought, No way. I need to figure a graceful way out. I offered to move some rocks, set up the tent, and collect water while the two of them climbed. I didn't mention that I would do a test run on my sleeping bag.

Early the next morning we packed up camp. Ascending the crumbly slope I felt stiff and sore. By necessity of the hunt, we moved slowly, searching each new vista for sheep. In mid-afternoon, we spotted a band of rams and crept toward them. Crouching behind dun-colored boulders, Eric and I watched John as he inched his way within shooting distance and took aim.

Shots echoed off the peaks a split second after the largest

ram's legs buckled from under him, then he tumbled over the far side of the ridge above us. I had no idea how far he'd fallen, but I'd done enough sheep hunting to know it could be a long distance. We climbed to join John, then descended through scree to where the sheep had come to rest on a patch of snow. After butchering the ram, we debated the merits of carrying our loads up a slide of loose and shifting rocks—sliding one step back for every two we made forward—or heading down an unknown drainage. We decided to go with the pull of gravity on our side.

With the weight from meat and horns equally divided in our packs, we headed down. Either the extra load narrowed the gap in our fitness levels or the descent helped me stay within sight of my partners. The valley narrowed and several chutes forced us to remove our loads and lower them one at a time. Rusted drums and twisted metal scraps occasionally poked through the rubble of the streambed. Those were good signs. If miners once carried heavy equipment up this stream, we should be able to make it down.

Along the stream's alder-choked lower reaches we bulled our way through twisted branches and devil's club. My bootlace came loose, but I kept going, afraid that if I bent over to tie it I would lose sight of John and Eric. I wasn't confident they would look back to see if I was still around.

My foot wobbled in my boot like a tire with loose lug nuts. Debris fell into the gap between leather and wool and pierced the fabric of my sock. I called for a time out. While tying my laces, I felt I was under the scrutiny of a stern scoutmaster. But maybe what I perceived as John's impatience was just an earnest hiker's fierce independence. I hadn't wanted to stop either, as I was feeling a bit stronger—almost as if the extra weight on my shoulders brought back some of the energy from my guiding days.

On the last slope to the lake, John said he needed some time to recharge before following the shoreline back to the canoe. I thought I detected a hint of weariness in his declaration. His minimalist approach to backcountry travel included the food he carried, yet he graciously offered some of his meager supply. Eric passed around jerky. I spread out my stash of candy bars and trail mix.

John was five years my senior, over fifty years old, and still one of the strongest hikers I'd met. I greatly admired his passion for fitness and knowledge of history, but the first real feeling of kinship came when he showed a bit of vulnerability. I felt generous and affable when John accepted the candy bar I offered. I wondered if his willingness to eat a snack laden with chocolate and refined sugar was a capitulation to fatigue. This was a man I'd seen balk at adding brown sugar to oatmeal, then turn around and eat cold spinach, straight from the can, for breakfast.

Sweat prickled the small of my back, slowly drying to an overall chill as we sat on a carpet of fragrant Labrador tea. Conversation thinned in a positive way, allowing my mind to stretch and rest in company with my quadriceps and calves. A faint, rosy light tinted the slopes and ridges of Copper Mountain, marking the close of a pre-solstice afternoon. We stood and shouldered our packs. I looked up from adjusting my waist belt to see John bound off like a spooked caribou. Apparently the sugar fix had kicked in. I instantly regretted the gift of candy. Along the shore John tramped, high stepping down a network of game trails, shouting out warnings to bears before entering each brushy draw.

The terrain inclined, forcing us onto a slope overlooking the water. A smattering of alders and other brush served as meager handholds, their purchase tenuous on the rocky soil. Our packs tested our balance, turning our movements into the bob and weave of punch-drunk fighters. At last we threw in the towel, caching our loads near the water's edge before continuing on. When we reached the spot where we had stashed the canoe, waves roughed the surface of the lake. As John and Eric prepared to paddle up to retrieve our packs, I began walking the lakeshore to Takoka Creek, where they would pick me up on their return.

Daylight diffused with a slow yawn into semidarkness as I worked my way along the beach. The wind freshened, shook the leaves and bent the crowns of spruce and birch. I was what some call, "good tired," when muscles ache so much they buzz and beg for rest because they have been reacquainted with their own design and purpose. My thoughts matched my pace, which was deliberate and deliciously mine alone.

At the mouth of Takoka Creek, I gathered driftwood and lit a fire. The light would serve as a beacon for John and Eric, who paddled toward me somewhere amid the waves and dusk. The surf swelled and broke with the din of falling stones. Wind forced its way through unseen branches in harsh whispers. It was a confusion of sounds, a bit jarring, having the ring of raw power.

Darkness settled fast. It seemed sensible to spend the night and cross the lake in the morning, but when the canoe appeared, John insisted we head to the island over a quarter-mile away, nearer the opposite shore. That was where he always camped.

I crawled into the middle of the overloaded canoe and sat on my pack. We angled through the rough water toward the island's lee without a single life vest between us. I glanced over my shoulder as John pulled his paddle hard and turned it sideways to guide our course.

Throughout this entire trip I had been at the mercy of forces over which I had little or no control: First the fog, turning me in circles, playing tricks and poking fun at me, reminding me that human plans and technologies are equally susceptible to failure; then the aspirations of a backcountry ironman, whose directional sense—forward!—was not always aligned with his companions'. I had relied on the boat's wake, hoping it would set me on a straight path; I had followed John's wake, wishing his internal GPS would experience something akin to a rollover day. Whatever the means of navigation, it was flawed, and I knew that, as American humorist and playwright George Ade put it: "No matter how many miles a man may travel, he will never get ahead of himself."

21

September Shadows

Early on the morning of September 10, 2001, I headed up the trail to Portage Creek. My father-in-law, Roy, planned to follow an hour later. For nine days he and I had been up bright and early hunting for moose. It was a still morning, and on the gentle rise to the summit I noticed an occasional fresh brown bear track. I passed by the ramshackle buildings of the Bowman gold mine and headed toward the log bridge over Portage Creek. An overgrown jeep trail that curves back and forth through a mixed forest of birch and spruce, it is a pathway I know well, comfortable and familiar as an old jacket. I moved slowly, glancing left and right looking for movement, a brown patch of hair, anything out of the ordinary. Bears had recently chewed and clawed two small spruce trees to mark their passing. Cranberries were plentiful and there were many grouse beds, but no fresh moose tracks.

Suddenly, on a corner where the trail turns right and drops out of sight, a brown bear sow and three two-year-old cubs appeared, walking briskly toward me. We locked eyes for an instant, then the sow stopped and glanced behind her to take account of her cubs.

Okay, Momma, just take 'em out of here, I said firmly.

She rose to three-quarters height, then dropped to all fours and lunged in my direction. The cubs followed, eagerly peering over their mother's shoulders. I had the feeling that whatever the sow wanted to do, attack or flee, they were up for the game. Each cub outweighed me, and even if the bears didn't have claws and teeth, their collective mass slamming into my body could flatten a man twice my size.

I braced for a tsunami of brown hair and muscle, then made a quick decision. I flicked off my rifle's safety and fired one shot over their heads. The sow veered slightly at the rifle's blast. The stampede of bruins rumbled by me at twenty feet and disappeared into the bushes.

Back at our cabin that night, still wound up from my experience, I turned on the radio to listen to the Bushlines, a message service for people without other forms of communication originating from a Homer public radio station. Anne received word from her mother that an editor from the East Coast wanted her to call him about a manuscript she'd entered in a poetry chapbook contest. "Strong winning possibilities," was the report. It was a small prize, but Anne was excited.

In the morning, we boated up to the neighbors so Anne could try using their satellite telephone to reach the editor. Chuck greeted us at the door. There was something ominous about the way he looked at us and the long pause before he spoke. "They've really done it now," he said. *Who has done what?* I thought.

Chuck and Sara welcomed us inside and we sat in a daze, sipping coffee and listening to the radio reports about the collapse of the World Trade Center. It all was so out of context to our wilderness existence that we didn't know what to make of it at first. Our lack of familiarity with New York City, our inability to name more than two skyscrapers worldwide, left us dumbfounded. But with the talk of hijacked jets, the Pentagon under attack, buildings collapsing into rubble, and comparisons to Pearl Harbor, the seriousness became clearer by the minute.

Anne halfheartedly punched in the numbers on the satellite phone. What a day to try to call New York! She finally got through, and after a protracted conversation was told, "Oh, by the way, congratulations." She had won.

I felt badly for Anne. She had worked hard for a little recognition from the literary world. Normally the grind of submissions and seemingly inevitable rejections overshadowed her successes. I wanted her to enjoy this rare victory. But the world, in its determination to show us just how insignificant we are, threw down a trump card. I understood. Just the night before, when adrenaline still coursed through my veins from the false charge, I wanted to relive the experience again, in the security of the cabin walls with Anne and Roy listening intently. I wanted to tell of other close calls and to dwell for a while inside the illusion that my encounter held some significance. Certainly one evening with an audience of two wasn't too much to ask.

I headed into the woods at first light on September 12. It wasn't just moose I was after, though I needed the meat. I felt stunned by the events back east and the endless radio news coverage. I needed something tangible, a reconnection with the natural world. At 9:30, near the edge of a beaver pond, a bull moose answered my call.

Roy and Anne heard the rifle's report. They threw knives and a saw in backpacks and headed up the trail to find me. The moose was down not far from our neighbor Howard's place. He was quick to help, and by mid-afternoon the four of us had all the meat on the beach in front of his cabin. Looking out at the wide expanse of water, we were apprehensive. An east wind carved the lake with whitecaps. Breakers pounded the shore. We accepted the loan of Howard's skiff powered by an old 50-horse outboard that Howard said was running "on three out of four cylinders." Heavily loaded, we plowed through the big waves, anticipating the protection of our own bay.

Well after dark I crawled in bed and quickly fell into a two-home-brew, no-intention-of-rising-early kind of a sleep. Anne lay snuggled next to me under the goose down comforter. Roy was ensconced down the hill in the old log cabin, a snorer's song away.

At 1:00 a.m. my sleep was interrupted with a protracted moan from outside and a sharp elbow in the ribs from Anne. "Did you hear THAT?" I clung to a heavy-eyed denial of the sound for a moment, wanting to bury my head under a pillow.

Shit, I thought. *A bear is in the meathouse!*

We stumbled onto the porch with flashlights, rifles, pots, and pans. There was a loud thrashing coming from the woods. We yelled and clanked, peering futilely into the dense growth. Soon the glow from a kerosene lamp shone through the old cabin window. We discussed the situation with Roy via brief shouts through the dark.

"Was that you?"

"No!"

"Can you see anything with the flashlight?"

"No!"

"What do you think we should do?"

"I don't know."

Minutes later, Anne and I carefully negotiated the single switchback trail down to the old cabin, listening for the crack of brush, watching for a blur of movement. I held a three-cell flashlight tightly against the forestock of my 30.06, the beam shinning down the barrel. Anne followed, an identical rifle in one hand, a flashlight in the other. When we reached the bottom of the hill, Anne and Roy covered me while I tipped a ladder onto the roof of the nearby shed and crawled on top. I still couldn't see the meathouse.

We regrouped inside the cabin. Anne, determined not to lose whatever was left of our meat, summoned our collective nerve. Huddled together we moved en masse to the beach, flashlights sweeping random patterns across the high grass and the trunks of poplar and spruce. On the beach in front of the meathouse we started a driftwood fire. I had never realized how much brush surrounded that little rough-cut structure. We waited some time before venturing up to the torn screen to look inside. The nail boards (eight penny nails hammered into pieces of half-inch plywood) that we had laid out to deter bears from breaking in were slightly out of place, and we knew the cause of the bear's moan. We peeked inside. Some of the meat that had been hanging on spikes and ropes from the rafters was gone. The rest lay in a pile on the gravel floor.

Standing in front of the shredded screen of the meathouse we chatted nervously and waited for first light. The fire occasionally flared up, casting a glow on the side of our Super Cub. With its faded yellow fabric and torn seat, it was the only airplane I had ever owned. It had served me well and was as much a friend as anything mechanical could be. It was strange that I could entertain positive thoughts about an airplane at the moment many people were thinking, maybe for the first time in their lives, of passenger jets, not as benign and convenient modes of transportation, but as deadly weapons—guided missiles of destruction.

When the radio reports said that all civilian flights were prohibited I couldn't believe they meant bush Alaska, where some of us have no other way to get to town. But it was true, even our two-place Super Cub would sit quietly on its trailer, grounded by a president I didn't vote for. I hadn't heard the sound of an airplane since we'd visited Chuck. It was eerie. The absence of flying things was a void in the sky, reminding me of the days following the 1964 Good Friday earthquake when the birds disappeared. I think my mother noticed it first. There was not a flurry or flash among the trees, not a chirp or trill anywhere. We prayed that the aftershocks would stop and the birds would start singing again, but we didn't talk about it much. I think we were all too frightened.

Roy paced around the driftwood fire's orbit of light. To pass the time, Anne began reading aloud from a Francine Prose novel, *Blue Angel*. The hollow texture to her voice was more than just exhaustion. This story of infidelity and the desire for recognition was dying of irrelevance on Anne's tongue. After a couple of pages, her voice trailed off to silence and she closed the book. I reached down and stroked the sleek black hair of our dog. What would tomorrow bring—for the world—for the three of us?

As I stood there, my disquietude spread. Although I had some influence on events in my immediate surroundings—maneuvering an open skiff in building seas or fending off bears in the dark—I had no control over world events. In the face of the September 11th tragedy, I was helpless. I couldn't fathom the terror those people on the airliners had experienced, the agony of their wait before the jets made impact.

I gripped the wooden stock of my rifle, felt the worn checkering. I ran my fingers over the smooth, steel ball on the bolt handle. The gun would protect me or not, depending on a mix of fortune and fortitude, the portions of each unknown and ever changing, like the shadows the fire cast around me. I slid the safety on my rifle forward and back, the small click punctuating the still night.

22

Of Wood and Warmth

One autumn evening I stepped into our bedroom addition to start a fire. I was still learning the personality of the stove, its ashes so new they barely covered half of the firebrick. As the flames flared up through the kindling, I realized I'd never owned a wood stove with a glass door before. I lay on the bed and watched the flickering, constantly reshaping brightness of the fire. The glow on the birch wood walls and the warmth gently shouldering its way toward the center of the room comforted me. The sight of the box of split spruce sitting nearby and the knowledge of stacks of firewood just outside the cabin door equaled those pleasures.

It isn't just the potential of wood as a reserve against cold and stormy times that intrigues me. The facets of forest and trees are many. I am fascinated by patterns—the rusty crowns of beetle-killed spruce standing out against deep forest green, the lazy twist of a trunk, a dead branch daubed with pale green and white moss. The intricacy of a tree's interior captivates: growth rings surrounding a darkened core like a target laid bare in the act of cutting. Sounds coming to my ears: frozen birch trees snapping under the weight of an unrelenting March snow, like gunshots across the bay.

A love of wood is in my blood. In 1950 my father was on his way from Wisconsin to Alaska when he ran out of money in northwest Montana. Inquiring about work, he and a partner were hired to cut trees. Using a two-man crosscut saw, they earned a hundred dollars an acre clearing pines above the site of the Hungry Horse Dam. From his experience, my father taught me not to push, but to pull in steady strokes in rhythm with one's partner, a similar saw. Later he showed me how to operate our raucous Homelite chainsaw. *Keep pumping the oiler with your thumb! Don't let the chain get loose!* He taught me to fell trees, to split and stack and age the wood. Never once did he mention this could become a lifelong passion.

Splitting is the most satisfying aspect of the labor involved in making firewood, especially the Bunyanesque feeling of power when splitting straight-grained birch during a cold spell. The wood flies away in clipped halves as if repelled from the steel. It is math, simple division: one stroke equals two pieces, over and over again.

Techniques for splitting wood are both learned and invented. Anne dislikes mauls and seldom employs a sledgehammer and wedges. Her axe of choice is one that belonged to local legend Brown Carlson, a trapper and miner originally from Norway, whose cabin still stands adjacent to ours. The year 1912 is stamped into the axe head; the handle was battered and chipped when we began using it. I was especially wary when I observed a technique that Brown had passed on to Anne's brothers, which they in turn taught her. When the axe was firmly embedded in a piece of wood, Brown would turn the axe and wood upside-down, swinging both above his head and strike them, axe head first, onto the splitting block. Brown (like Anne and the axe itself) was small and well built. Though the technique looks far from safe, it is very effective, putting weight and momentum on the side of someone not born with bulk. Anne couldn't bear to re-place the smooth, sweat-soaked handle until we had to, and it's still sound a decade later. The new handle I purchased years ago sits in our shed waiting its turn.

I like to believe I have eclectic tastes when it comes to choosing a tool to split wood. If the piece is small I'll use Brown's axe, being extra cautious so the handle doesn't break on my watch. A larger piece can be divided by striking a line of blows from edge to edge or by taking slices off the out-side, changing the shape from round to a smaller and small-er polygon. For unruly chunks, I'll wrap my hands around a maul and use it like a muscled axe to impose my will on the wood. Often I halve or quarter the pieces with the maul, then switch to the axe to finish the work.

Obstinate pieces require special treatment. Driving steel wedges in with a sledgehammer may seem like bully work that could blast through anything. Not true. If knots aren't avoided or a wedge is driven into a punky section of fire-wood, the wedge can become hopelessly buried. Wedges have different shapes and weights. Some enter the wood easily, while others need the score of an axe as a starting point. In combination, wedges work well together, to widen a split or help remove a stuck wedge or axe.

I inspect, sometimes overtly, sometimes covertly, my neigh-bors' woodsheds. It is a way of comparing and caring. Do they have enough for the winter? Spruce or birch? I look to see how closely the branches are trimmed, if the wood is split or still in rounds. Are the pieces stacked neatly or in a haphazard fashion? When I walk by my brother-in-law's pile of tinder-dry, straight-grained wood I feel both jealou-sy and pride.

Perhaps ironically, having many stoves to feed makes wood cutting easier. If a piece is too long, it is saved for the barrel stove. Big, gnarly chunks go in the bathhouse stove with the large door. Bent pieces that don't stack well get burned in the sauna. Straight-grained sections are divided up to fit stoves in the addition or kitchen, or hauled to the guest cabin. The best wood is pared down to kindling.

That's not the end of it. Ashes mixed with dead, spawned-out salmon fertilize the garden or are returned to the forest floor. The chips of bark that encircle the chopping block are spread as mulch in the garden to keep weeds down. Lake ice is stored under piles of sawdust for summer use. I love this continuum of spruce, birch, and poplar.

A friend once told me that fifteen percent of a healthy forest is dying. When trees past their prime are harvested instead of robust ones, more wood is required to provide an equal amount of heat, and ashes must be cleaned from the stoves with greater frequency.

The smugness Anne and I once felt about our self-proclaimed "wise" use of resources has transformed into an appreciation and awareness of a cycle that has little to do with us. It doesn't take much study to see that the forest floor is made up largely of the forest itself. Leaves and needles rain down; mature trees snap and uproot; mosses, lichens, fungi, and seedlings network over and within the natural compost. Although terms like mycelium and mycorrhiza may never be part of my working vocabulary, the existence of an amazing interconnection is clear enough. It would be a disaster to rob a forest of all of its dead and dying—to clean away the rot entirely is to clean away life. What allows Anne and me our own version of selective cutting is our incredible fortune to live in a place of few people and many trees. Each harvest is a series of choices.

I eyed the swaybacked birch for years, watching it slouch closer to the earth. Eighteen inches across at the base, the tree was not damaged or beginning to rot. Growing near a small creek, it had fought hard to maintain an upright position. But its vertical will was nothing against the force of gravity. When I cut it down, I experienced that familiar tinge of guilt that comes from slicing into a solid tree. I tried to halve the first sections to make them easier to lift, but the axe bounced off the wood like a bug plunking off a windshield. As I cut lengths, Anne rolled the pieces onto a sled and pulled them across the snowy ground to a nearby trail. We stacked the wood under our cache.

The first piece I tried to split resisted my efforts. I searched for a weakness, a starting point. The axe, then the maul, rebounded off the surface, leaving scars in spoke patterns. Every stroke produced the same result: bounce, bounce, bounce. I set the piece back under the cache and waited for colder weather. March did not disappoint, offering many frigid days. Even at twenty degrees below zero, the wood repulsed the steel as if this particular tree was a birch-rubber hybrid.

Anne and I, working in turns, didn't exactly split, but tore, small sections from the perimeter of a round. The inside of the pieces revealed a confused grain, running in the shape of a lazy s, each line sporting a tight zigzag that was visually interesting but hell on the body. We hacked at one or two pieces a day for three weeks until the tree was divided into a hodgepodge of shapes and sizes.

Food. Shelter. Warmth. Why is it that the more my life re-volves around basic needs, the wealthier I feel? When I was caretaking a lodge in the Alaska Range, Red Beeman, a guide with his own operation down the range, stopped in occa-sionally on flights to town. One cool fall day, before step-ping into the cabin for coffee and conversation, Red poked his head in the lean-to to study my woodpile. Dry spruce rounds lined the enclosure from end to end. He turned to face me, an elfish delight ablaze in his eyes. "Just like mon-ey in the bank!" he chirped, his ruddy cheeks barely able to contain a huge grin.

I believe now that Red viewed the firewood as a real, phys-ical representation of security. I think about the Sarayacu people of Ecuador defending their forest home from devel-opers with palmwood lances; about environmental writer Janisse Ray's passion for the strong and resinous longleaf pine of Georgia; about Joe Stevens, a Koyukon Athabaskan whose reverence for birches extends to cutting the thin-nest slice from a tree to check the straightness of its grain—a slice so thin that the tree, if not felled, can heal without being harmed. I think of these people and their actions, and I know that beyond my own leaf-and-needle horizon, I have kin.

Walking through the woods near our cabin I am sur-rounded by seedlings, trees, and deadfalls. An incense of evergreen and Labrador Tea spices the air. Bark settles be-neath my feet. I am home.

23

Salvage

Ice—good traveling for humans and animals—a highway, a shortcut, sometimes, a trap. Water—the liquid state of ice, the mask beneath the mask, life itself, and sometimes, death.

It was a cold spring for southwest Alaska, with freezing nighttime temperatures occasionally dropping to single digits, preserving winter well into April. The day we found her—Sunday, the 27th—began below freezing but quickly warmed by a brilliant sun to the forties.

Though Lake Clark was still locked in ice, the afternoon air finally felt warm. After a morning of writing I cleaned out the swallow houses and organized boxes of tools and hardware in the old cabin—two rites of spring that at last seemed justified.

Late that afternoon Anne and I took our dog Zipper for a walk. We are often inclined to travel east because terrain provides protection from the prevalent strong winds blowing out of the pass. But the day was calm and we headed west. A light snow the day before had textured the ice perfectly for hiking—no slip or slush or deep drifts. Three quarters of a mile into our walk we noticed a dark spot on the otherwise white, frozen expanse. A pressure crack had opened up a month before during warm, windy weather, but had since refrozen.

Normally nothing would be odd about a pressure crack reopening this time of year, as wind and rapid temperature changes force the ice on each side of these cracks to shear and grind like tectonic plates. But the cool, stable conditions and the fact that the crack appeared open in only one spot caught our attention. Then I remembered a pair of moose we'd seen two weeks before, traveling only a mile away from where we stood.

"I bet a moose fell through the ice," I said to Anne, and we altered our course to inspect. As we neared the five-by-forty foot hole I held to hopes that because the opening was narrow, the animal had managed to extricate itself. But when we got closer we saw the motionless body of a cow moose floating in the hole. One ear was bird-pecked down to cartilage, and strands and chunks of hair were scattered about. We circled the hole and found tracks of another moose zigzagging around its perimeter, heading in an irregular pattern toward shore. There were no bear tracks, or signs of wolves, coyotes, or wolverine—just a literal earmark of the first winged wave of scavengers.

A biologist had told me the moose population in this area is small yet stable, with an adequate bull to cow ratio. But living here year-round and talking with other locals who observe moose both from the air and the ground, I thought his assessment overly optimistic. I had seen only three different moose in the past seven months. Now one was dead.

Anne asked me when I thought the drowning had occurred. I studied the clues. Tracks and hair were clearly visible, and had not been dusted with any fresh snow. Newly formed skim ice varnished the open water in shimmering patches. I told Anne it had likely taken place less than twenty-four hours earlier. Later, she would recall how the previous afternoon Zipper had barked his big-animal bark and locked his attention westward across the ice to something we couldn't see or hear.

"We should salvage the meat," Anne insisted. Yes, I thought, that is the practical thing to do, perfectly aligned with our philosophies and our subsistence lifestyle. But we live in a national park and preserve, and our subsistence rights, though liberal, are regulated by the federal government. This moose didn't belong to us. A spirited debate regarding our next course of action followed. I teased Anne that she leaned toward knives first, permission later.

Our compromise was to document everything with photos, pull the moose onto the surface of the ice and contact the park requesting permission to proceed with butchering. After shooting photos from all angles, we lassoed the moose around the neck with a stout rope then anchored our four-wheeler with an ice screw. I stretched out the winch cable from the front of the machine to the moose. Anne operated the winch, taking in the cable, but the moose's bulk stopped on the lip of the ice. I tugged on a front leg and the cow slid onto the surface, icy water dripping from her slick hair.

"Let's pull her in front of our cabin so wolves or bears won't get *our* moose," Anne pleaded. I noticed the possessive, and recognized that she was half joking—but only half.

Anne wrote an impassioned letter summarizing our discovery, stressing our desire to use this unexpected gift of protein. I attached images to the email and we sent it to Joel Hard, the Park Superintendent, late that evening. It seemed ironic or perhaps even a bit sacrilegious to be using such technology to instantly communicate our wish to subsist from the land. This hands-in-blood versus hands-on-keyboard marriage made me uneasy. It was a dovetailing of the old and new that would not have been possible for us four years before. Anne and I convert slowly to the latest and greatest. We had resisted purchasing the four-wheeler with its powerful winch for years, and computer and Internet hookup took even longer.

The first thing Monday morning Joel gave us permission to begin the salvage. He said he would send a ranger in a few days to gather more information. I was surprised. I had expected the bureaucratic wheels to become high-centered on a desk, awaiting interpretation by someone in Washington DC of an obscure regulation known only by numbers on each side of a decimal point. Yet here was Joel with a courteous, prompt, practical response. It was time to sharpen knives and grab the meat saw. We pulled the cow across the ice to the middle of our bay and stopped at a spot we could see from our cabin.

I haven't gutted a large animal in the traditional manner in years. Most people make cuts up the belly to the neck, split the sternum and pelvis, and reach arm's length into the chest cavity to cut the contents free and pull out the entrails and organs. With large animals it is messy and uncertain work, hands and forearms submerged in blood. Years ago I was shown how to approach from the side, to skin one half of the animal starting at the backbone, then remove all the meat from that side first. Gravity pulls the entrails away from the rib cage, and once the ribs are removed, everything can be cut away cleanly and rolled from the carcass. Then the animal is turned over, allowed to drain of blood for a few minutes, and skinned and butchered on the other side.

I made the initial cuts, Anne grabbed a knife, and together

we peeled back the hide. Anne isn't fond of cold or wind, but she shifts into a different gear at times like this, becoming even tougher and more pragmatic than usual, engaging in the work with a relaxed confidence. She muscled-over the top front shoulder, then the hind ham, as I cut them free. I boned the meat from half of the neck and cut out the top backstrap.

When we first pulled the cow out of the water the roundness of her abdomen made me think she was pregnant. After the effects of a cool night on her body I wasn't so sure. I ran my hand across the taut flesh of her freshly skinned belly. I felt something hard, like a head or hooves. My knife slit the abdominal wall just below the rib cage and a bulging sac with spidery, surface veins forced its way into the cool morning air. It rolled to the ice and lay like a misshapen bloodshot eye or a grotesque jellyfish. I fingered the sac and felt the shapes of two calves. Wishing to postpone dealing with the discovery, we rolled it to the side and finished butchering the cow.

Later, we opened the sac—the chorion, I would learn eventually—and another, a thin, interior one. Serous fluid flowed out, collapsing the amniotic membrane around the tiny bodies. The calves were fully formed except the tips of their hooves, which were soft and yellow.

The randomness of it all seemed vastly unfair. The moose this cow was traveling with was a young bull. A cow took one misstep, a bull walked free. Three moose died instead of one—a tough blow in an area where the moose population is far from robust.

The fetuses were slick and brown, curled as if sleeping. A

true subsistence user would get over his squeamishness and take the calf meat too, but I hesitated mentioning the idea to Anne. I recalled when we faced a similar decision. The memory of my own hollow-stomached sadness and Anne's tears returned. It was three years ago in May. Zipper had inadvertently chased a calf into the lake. The water that time of year is not much above freezing, maybe thirty-eight degrees at most—a temperature that proved lethal for a newborn calf. Months passed after the incident before words helped Anne purge some of her grief. She titled her poem "Dirge":

> I carried the moose calf back
> along our beach, where the rocks
> are large enough to make me stumble.
>
> I carried her back—
> I judged her the weight
> of a small dark cloud—
> she was one week old, at most.
>
> I tried at first
> to purge the water
> from her lungs, her nose.
>
> The calf dashed into our yard
> separated from her mother
> —a bear between them, we figured—
>
> then swam too far
> in the frigid lake
> chased by my Border collie pup,
> who only wanted to play.

Settled In

When she finally turned,
we heard her whimpers.
Her ears were down,
her swimming slower.

I carried her back from where
she'd almost managed the shore.
I was not even sure if she drowned
or died from shock.

I should have run when I first saw her
toppling like a body gone with drink,

should have pulled her from the water
toweled her coat, offered
a bottle of warm sweet milk.

We thought the mother dead,
the calf just resting
in the shallows.

And what would we have done
with the mother gone
and the tiny thing in a pen—
our own exotic zoo?

I carried the moose calf back
while another question
shaded the foundering, midday sun—
should we eat her?

We laid her down
on our boat's red carpet.
She was such a beautiful, simple brown
her eyes a little milky,
oval as a murre's.

On the smallest island we left her
in alder on the dusty ground.
There was never a fleck of blood.

The mother was standing
when we returned
in water up to her knees.

She did not run
or make a sound,
her head was up

while mine, for days, it hung, it hung,
and my tears were loud
but they were not good.

That was one moose I didn't have the stomach to eat—I talked Anne out of it. Maybe I wasn't hungry enough, or perhaps it was the thought of complicity. Our dog, our fault. But this time we didn't have the excuse of our dog's playfulness backfiring to stop us. We were simply witnesses, just a couple of scavengers in a land of many.

Without any prompting from me, Anne broached the idea of utilizing the meat from the calves. We seemed to realize it was senseless not to use this gift of bonus meat—many day's worth of meals for us. The decision was quick and practical, but not easy. As we skinned and gutted, I thought of subsistence as a job you love, but don't always like. We did our job.

A west wind freshened across the ice of the bay. Our fingers became stiff and cold in the breeze. I just wanted to be finished, and imagined we were dressing out a couple of dik-dik, the small African antelope I had read about that are often used as camp meat. It helps sometimes to create a buffer between mind and hand.

As I finished with knife and saw and cleaned a few random hairs from the pieces we'd cut, Anne pulled the quarters, ribs, and boned meat of the cow to shore. It took her seven trips, skidding a small sled across the ice. Wrestling slippery chunks up to the meat house rafters, we tied them side-by-side until the tiny structure filled to capacity. Though the morning temperatures still felt like winter, the calendar and the daylight indicated that it was bear season. We surrounded the structure with an electric fence.

That night, along with rice and corn, we ate two tiny hearts. Each one fit easily in the palm of my hand, like an undersized baseball. They tasted much like hearts of other animals I have eaten: caribou, deer, elk, bison, and sheep, but they were a bit more tender.

Several days passed before we tried to eat meat from one of the young. The flesh was pale and fatty, soft, with a rubbery texture. As I chewed the never-worked muscles, each piece felt like something foreign in my mouth, with all the appeal of Vienna sausages after a seven-course meal. We both pushed our plates away and looked at each other. The following morning, we carried the calves' bodies out on the ice to leave for the birds and other critters. Sharing is sometimes an act of generosity, sometimes a gift for the giver.

Some of the cow meat we shared with neighbors, most of whom only wanted small amounts. These were our nearest neighbors, four to fourteen miles distant, who either didn't own a freezer or had one that was already full of berries and salmon. All the meat that we couldn't eat fresh would be pressure-canned on our wood cookstove.

For ten days—all day, every day—we processed meat. We boned and trimmed it. We ground it by hand and browned it in skillets on the stove. We hauled armloads of split spruce and birch, fed the fire, and heated water. We washed jars, packed them, and loaded them into the canner. And we ate: tenderloin, burger, ribs, and roasts. It was a protein-saturated race with the meat-souring spring weather that was sure to finally arrive.

Our cabin, our clothes, my mustache, smelled like a soup kitchen. Our main escape was to look out the window. At the bone pile, ravens, eagles, and an occasional magpie feasted on the hide, hooves, and backbone we'd left them—and the daily additions of trimmings and bones we offered. The birds eyed one another cautiously, cawed, shrieked, jumped, and flew in wing-aided hops, maintaining varying distances from one another.

A wolf visited the scrap pile twice. Anne insists it was two wolves. She claims the second wolf was darker in color and slightly larger than the first one. I counter that the difference in daylight at the time of the sightings made the same animal appear darker—and to her, larger. Nothing can be proved, but we both are convinced we are right—or at least we were to begin with. I think our own personal truth of the moment has been weakened by the other's insistence. We continue the debate for the sport of it—a chess match that no one can lose.

That there was just one wolverine, visiting three times, we agree. We watched it lope in a wide circle around the bay on its first approach. It carried off hooves and leg bones to the protection of the trees, some pieces so large the wolverine had to drop them every fifteen or twenty feet to secure another grip. The diamond-shaped markings on its back rippled as its compact, muscled body tipped the entire back-bone up to gnaw the vertebrae with its powerful jaws.

For years, in the 1970s and '80s, my father and uncle joined a few friends on annual weeklong trips to ice fish in the Lake Louise area near Glennallen. They caught huge burbot and lake trout, and speared whitefish. It was often brutal-ly cold, even in March, and the ice in most places was three feet thick. I joined them a couple of times but missed the year of the cow moose.

That year on a morning trip to check their sets in a treach-erous spot between Tyone Lake and Susitna Lake, they found a cow moose treading water in an open hole. The underwa-ter currents, the slow flow between lakes, often caused over-flow and unreliable ice conditions. The exhausted moose tried to avoid the fishermen closing in on her. She couldn't get far. Someone managed to loop a rope around her neck and steer her to the ice edge. When her front hooves struck the solid surface the men heaved together on the rope and pulled her free. With some difficulty they removed the rope and the cow rested, then wandered off into the surround-ing hills of stunted black spruce.

I think about the moose my father rescued and imagine what would have happened if Anne and I had walked west a day earlier, or possessed our dog's hearing to catch distant whimpers and splashes bouncing weakly across the ice. A step, a direction, sometimes changes everything: newborn calves suckling their mother, animals and birds searching hungrily for food; or cases of meat stored beneath a cabin's floor, the wildlife sleeping off its feast, traces of bones, hair, and hide drifting out of our bay on rotting ice, then sinking like shadows into the blue-green depths of the lake.

Afterword

Alaska was a territory when I was born. Growing up in Anchorage in the 1950s and '60s, my physical world was defined not by ivy-covered brownstones and paved streets but by handcrafted homes, gravel roads, forests, rivers, and mountains. As a child, all the fish, grouse, moose, and caribou we harvested were trophies, regardless of size, though we made a good-natured game of who caught or shot the biggest, the first, or the most. It wasn't much different in the garden. Mom, Dad, and I would dig with spade and hands in the potato patch hoping to be the one to pull out the largest spud or the greatest number on one plant. Spuds and carrots in the root cellar, wild meat in the freezer, cranberry juice, and raspberry jam: it was all part of a bountiful harvest, inseparable and good.

Signs of a hunting culture were everywhere. Antlers adorned the walls of houses, cabins, garages, and sheds. The practice was so common that I never thought twice about it. Antlers and horns had functional purposes as well. They were used as doorknobs, towel racks, table legs, and chairs; they became lamps, jewelry, and knife handles; they were placed in rock gardens as ornaments. They were the rusty anchors of seaside ports; the wagon wheels of western towns.

When I was in my early twenties, my justification for guiding trophy hunters was simple: it was an excuse to be in the wilderness, and it provided food for my family and me.

All edible game was properly salvaged, cared for, and consumed with pleasure. Many hunters chose to leave at least a portion of the meat with their guide. So what began as one person's quest for a trophy ended as nourishment, lean but hearty, the rich vegetation that had passed through the animal's body absorbed again in my own flesh.

Sadly, meat taken from the wild is not always utilized. Even the most accepted kind of hunter—the subsistence user—is sometimes wasteful. I've heard stories of whale and caribou steaks tossed out in the spring due to over-harvest. Freezer-burned fish routinely discarded because it was improperly wrapped. Carcasses of walrus, moose, sheep, and bison left to rot because they would have had to be carried too far.

It is still difficult for me to divide the pursuit of game into the well-defined categories of meat and trophy hunting.

There is so much more to a hunt than that fraction of time it takes to pull the trigger. Although I never set out to become a guide (rather, I just fell into it), I found the freedoms and challenges of the job intoxicating: climbing mountains, crossing snow bridges, and exploring hanging valleys. I would sit on a hillside surrounded by plump blueberries, stained fingers holding binoculars, elbows braced on my knees, my thoughts rising up like heat waves above a shale slope on an August afternoon. I would plan and dream: explore Lynx Creek tomorrow, and the day after, the Earl River. I would gauge my clients' and my own abilities. Was this ridge too steep or that river crossing too swift?

More than once, peering over a rock or bush at an animal grazing contentedly nearby, I wondered how I might live this life, experience such wonder, without having to shatter the stillness with the blast of a rifle.

To shoot with a camera instead of a gun entered my thoughts. But I understood photography enough to realize that it took even more patience and luck than hunting. Though a camera rode in my pack almost every day, I didn't have the skill or the inclination to succeed as a professional. It's true that when the index finger clicks a shutter an animal doesn't die. Still, it is not a "clean" occupation and it was less so in the decades I was guiding. In *Tracks of the Unseen* Nick Jans confesses that he exposed 180 slides on just one trip, all destined for the trash. He does not address the chemicals and minerals used in production and the energy required to manufacture and transport camera gear to market and photographers to their destinations. Even with the overwhelming conversion from film to digital, photography continues to exact a toll on the environment.

Camera parts settling into landfills here in America or in third world countries don't tend to assault the senses like the image of a rotting bear carcass. But considering the sustainability of a limited harvest of game animals and the fact that bears, foxes, wolves, and birds feed on the remains, which also leech nutrients into the soil, I don't feel qualified to judge one pursuit less morally acceptable than another.

Other careers held even less appeal. I had watched geologists in the Alaska Range getting daily helicopter rides to alpine country that would have taken me days to reach. The geologists were a fit and intelligent lot, returning each day with packs full of rock samples. But they were scouts for future mining activity. If, when, and to what degree scars would be laid upon the land was unknown even to them. They stayed in lodges or neat tent camps and supped on corn-fed beef, French wine, and imported beer.

It wasn't that I thought my profession was better than others, but I realized that the activities of the photographer, geologist, and big game guide all, to one degree or another, have adverse impact on the land and resources. Even biologists, under the cover of species' protection, cause stress to animals. State and federal employees use fixed-wing aircraft and fuel-guzzling, deafening helicopters to count birds' nests. They anaesthetize and tranquilize, install radio tracking devices and other foreign equipment around the necks of ungulates or in the gullets of fish. I've seen moose with skin rubbed hairless from chafing collars—collars that sometimes serve as a lethal claw-hold for brown bear.

My hunters came from many backgrounds and professions. I guided oil executives, physicians, professional athletes; a fence contractor, an FBI agent, and a lingerie manufacturer. Some had saved for years for the trip of a lifetime; others were multi-millionaires for whom the cost of the hunt was pocket change.

Many hunters approached their trip as a multifaceted adventure. They marveled at the wilderness around them, moving with and through the land. They took time to notice the small things: alpine arnica, king boletes, mourning-cloak butterflies, dark-eyed juncos. Sore muscles and damp socks were endured with good humor, considered modest user fees gladly paid.

But for some the objective of a trip was simply a trophy to be secured as quickly as possible. What was important was that they came home with a moose "bigger than Uncle Bob's" or that their name be immortalized in *Boone and Crockett* or *Safari Club International* record books. The value of an animal's life, a week or two of fresh air and exercise on mountains, ridges, and lakes were reduced to a number, a score, a swagger, or a brag.

More than once I watched a hunter's grim countenance as I stretched a tape measure across a rack or around a set of horns. If his standard of excellence had not been met—sixty inches wide for moose, thirty-eight inches of curl for a Dall ram, for example—then the hunt was, to himself, a failure.

As the years went by and I began attending hunters' conventions and visiting the homes of a few clients, a sense of unease took hold in me. I saw high-ceilinged trophy rooms; walls lined with rugs and pelts; shoulder, half-mounts, and life-sized reproductions in corners or on artificial ledges, the spaces in between filled with birds and small game. Blank spots on the wall were explained in an apologetic tone, as if the vacancy were a blemish on the hunter's self-worth.

I wondered how and when the shift occurred, from hanging a single rack on a shed to constructing a personal museum containing fifty or a hundred species. I learned that competition brings out the worst in us: pride, covetousness, and envy.

"Appropriate and compassionate behavior toward nature." Ted Kerasote, author of *Bloodties* and *Heart of Home*, uses these words to define Aldo Leopold's idea of "the land ethic." What does it mean to me?

Certainly some baselines are easy to establish pertaining to hunting: not to scar up the country with motorized vehicles or use them to drive, herd, harass, or molest game; not to litter or hunt endangered or threatened species or damage habitat; to salvage all edible meat, to always strive for a clean shot, and to consider taking animals that are past their prime.

Zurückgesetzt is the term German hunters use when antlers "set back" or begin to revert. For moose this typically occurs after the age of ten or twelve. The rack doesn't grow as wide; the palms narrow and become thick. Sometimes odd projections hang down or point up, and bases are bulbous or misshapen. It is part of the German hunter's heritage to revere an animal in the final stages of life—more honorable to shoot an old one than one with a larger and more symmetrical rack. I don't know the origin of the practice, but the result is a wise conservation measure that targets older animals in lieu of ones still in their optimum years for breeding.

Hunters often defend hunting as a quest to return to a closer interaction with nature or as the expression of an ancient urge to provide. But hunters and nonhunters alike distance themselves more all the time from the intricate web of life to which we are all linked. People look at mountains through a lens, follow dotted lines on a GPS screen, head into the woods with cell phones instead of savvy. I like to think there is a way for hunters to re-establish the sense of connectedness to the natural world that they claim to desire.

I imagine what would happen if we did away with record books, which have only been around for a little over a hundred years. Perhaps the notion of a hunt as *sport* would fade and we would again become students of the plants, animals, air, water, and earth that sustain us. Better-educated hunters who understand their duties regarding ecosystem management, ethics, and wilderness preservation would cast hunting in a better light.

It has been over fifteen years since I've guided a hunter. I gave up guiding in part because the industry was going the same way most business ventures go in America: they squeeze out the small-time operator. Costs were increasing rapidly, and my time in the field with clients was decreasing. I was spending more time at conventions, with correspondence, and in my airplane. The experience was turning into a competition with other guides—too often a foot race up the mountains.

Regulations changed, eliminating exclusive guide areas. The change allowed guides more mobility, but also made it possible for the greedy to overharvest one particular area, then move to another. The incentive for guides to get to know an area intimately, to adjust their harvest to changing game populations for the long-term benefit of both themselves and the animals, was diminished. No longer could a guide decide not to hunt in a drainage or section of mountains for several years so it could rebound naturally. Someone would likely move in quickly and the area would never get a rest.

There were other reasons I quit. Two herniated disks in my lower spine made the physical demands difficult. I felt at times that the game was more venerable than the hunter. Too often I was rooting for the animal to get away, torn with the knowledge that it was my skill and experience that tipped the scales the other way.

Still, I can't discount all the claims hunters make to support their endeavor: that hunting is a significant part of the economy, that dollars from license and tag fees contribute to habitat preservation and wildlife conservation, that death from a well-placed bullet is less cruel than one from starvation, disease, or attacks from predators.

I have few regrets about my time spent guiding. What I learned about my own physical and emotional limitations and the outdoor savvy I gained enhanced my life beyond measure. Some say that all trophy hunters are scum. I know differently, but I found I had less in common with my clients as the years went by. To me, the guiding and the hunting were part of being an Alaskan. It was my identity and my sense of place.

Many memories from my guiding days remain vivid—some are grand adventures, others are vest-pocket poignancies. Looking out at the Chigmit Mountains from my present home, I am easily transported back to the Teocallis, where I spent the bulk of my guiding career. Again I feel the straps of my pack snug against my shoulders, my hip boots folded below my knees, the sweat in the small of my back evaporating with a pleasant coolness. An incommensurable power surrounds me, as if I am protected and exposed at the same time. A buttress of variegated gray rock rises on my left, obscuring the mountains beyond, its stratum slightly tilted, curving up and out of sight. To my right, a steep incline plunges down in alternating swaths of loose rubble and grass to the waters of a snowmelt creek. Deep ravines tattoo the mountains with nearly vertical cuts. On the far side of the drainage, steep ridges sickle and slash their way to a dominating summit that towers above the brown gray mass of talus at its base.

Those moments, when I stood, gazing out in sheer admiration of the country, without an animal in sight, were enough.

Acknowledgments

I want to thank all the friends, family, guides, and hunters I have shared time with in the outdoors. Even though your name may not appear in these pages, my life would have been diminished without your companionship and our adventures together. A few individuals who have endured more of me-in-the-wilds than most: Hal Orth, Jerry Ondola, Tom Springer, Gary Rogers, Jim Baski, Scott Quist, Are Strom, Allen Ah You, Bob Cook, Wesley Reed, Carlton Erikson, and of course, my parents, Gus and Ann Kahn, and my wife, Anne Coray.

I have been fortunate beyond measure to spend time with three of the most fiercely independent and skilled outdoorsmen Alaska will ever know: Vic Lenhart, and the late Stan Frost and Jay Hammond.

Thanks to the Rasmuson Foundation for a project grant to work on this book. I am indebted to Jay Hammond who liked my words enough to send a story of mine to *Alaska* magazine without my knowledge (which was subsequently published) and to Nancy Lord for support that came at a critical time. Thanks to everyone at the University of Nebraska Press, especially Rob Taylor and Katie Neubauer.

I owe a debt of gratitude to Sue Goodglick, a friend on both sides of the mountains, who saved me a long flight to the copy store, and to Tom Gage, who saved my life in Seward. Thanks to the generous folks who provided critiques of individual stories in this collection: Mike Burwell, Dan May,

Gail Coray, Craig Coray, and Claudine Wright. Special appreciation is owed to both Anne Coray and Glenn Wright, whose deft editing and tireless efforts to polish my rough words into a whole can never be fully repaid. I am in awe of your talents!

Anne, I couldn't have done it without you.

Several of these essays originally appeared, some in slightly different form, in the following magazines and journals. Thanks to the editors and publishers who printed my work:

Alaska magazine:

"Of Wood and Warmth," October 2009
"Burn," May 2008
"Almost Too Legal," August 2007
"Standing on a Heart," February 2006
"A Face in the Fog," September 2003
"The Hard Way Home," March 2002

Pilgrimage, vol. 32, (1), 2007: "One Last Cast"

ISLE: Interdisciplinary Studies of Literature and Environment, Winter 2007: "Crabbing"

Red Mountain Review, Fall 2005: "Return"

Friends: Stories of Friendship, Michaeline Della Fera and Linda Watskin, editors. Hollis: A Measure of Words Press, 2005: "Field Test," "Hats off to Hal" (a short version)

"Standing on a Heart" was also published in:

Crosscurrents North: Alaskans on the Environment, Holleman and Coray, editors. Fairbanks: University of Alaska Press, 2008
Wild Moments, Michael Engelhard, editor. Fairbanks: University of Alaska Press, 2009: appeared as "Heart Underfoot"

To order or obtain more information on these
or other University of Nebraska Press titles,
visit www.nebraskapress.unl.edu.